THE KINGFISHER

ROSEMARY EASTMAN

The Kingfisher

COLLINS

ST JAMES'S PLACE, LONDON

1969

TO GREGOR MACKENZIE

Contents

Illustrations

I

The Kingfisher's Home

THE KINGFISHER is surely one of the most beautiful birds in Britain. Certainly it is the only one of its family (Alcedinidae) resident here. It is quite different in shape from any other species, except perhaps the woodpecker, and in brilliant colouring it outdoes all our other more sombrely clad birds. Its strict diet of fish keeps it forever busy on the quiet backwaters of our rivers and other fresh waters, so that it is seldom seen. Tennyson called it 'the secret splendour of the brooks.'

At first we had no intention of studying the bird in detail. It was merely another brilliant subject for a nature film Ron was making on the River Test. Later, when the bird became less elusive and as we grew familiar with its main haunts and found that it had very rarely been successfully photographed, its fishing habits and breeding biology began to fascinate us, and the idea of filming it more fully became something of a challenge.

As our obsession with kingfishers grew, so the measures we took to watch them and to find out their

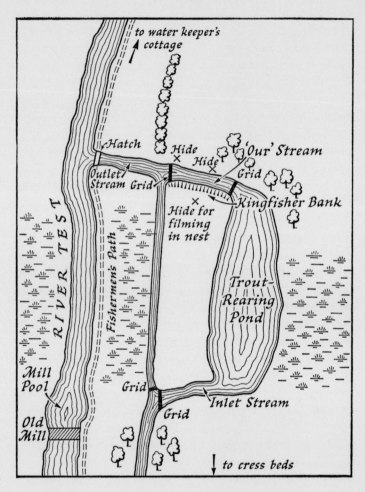

'The streams of the River Test were the Kingfisher'
territory'

favourite fish became more elaborate. We went to great lengths to get them to perform and breed before the camera, and even tried to help them survive by making sure that our 'kingfisher bird table' was abundant with fish not only at the times when we wanted to film them around and in it, but in bad weather too. Later, having gained a good deal of knowledge on how young kingfishers were brought up, we were able to hand-rear six abandoned youngsters ten days old, a feat that had seldom been successfully achieved. Perhaps this was something by way of repayment to the species we had so long exploited.

Kingfishers belong to the order Coraciiformes, land birds living in sub-tropical and tropical regions. The chief characteristic of these birds is their syndactyl feet—the three front toes are joined for part of their length. Other similar features are the structure of the palate bone, the form of the leg muscles and the way the tendons are joined to them, and the feather distribution and tract arrangement.

With a few exceptions Coraciiformes are very colourful birds with striking bills. The size of the birds varies greatly from the very small $3\frac{1}{2}$ inch todies to 5 foot hornbills. They are cavity nesters, are noisy rather than musical, and mostly carnivorous. Their eggs, which are white or slightly coloured, are rarely marked and usually number between three and six.

The young are born blind and naked and are reared in the nest. Kingfishers can be found in both the Old and New Worlds. Coraciiformes are divided into seven well-defined families: kingfishers, todies, motmots, bee-eaters, rollers, hoopoes and wood hoopoes, and hornbills. Kingfishers are divided into two sub-

families: the Alcedininae include the familiar fishing
kingfishers found throughout the world, and the
Daceloninae comprise the forest kingfishers, which are
more primitive, larger and more diversified—an Old
World group who often live far from water. The fishing kingfishers have long, narrow, sharp-pointed bills,
whereas those of the forest kingfishers are broader,
flatter and sometimes hooked at the tip. Best-known
and most widespread of the fishing kingfishers are the
Common Kingfisher (*Alcedo atthis ispida* Linnaeus) of
the Old World and the Belted Kingfisher (*Megaceryle
alcyon*) of the New World. The Common Kingfisher is
Europe's only species, and is the subject of this book.
Altogether there are eighty-four living species of kingfishers, found on every continent except in the polar
regions. They are of ancient lineage; their fossil
record, of which there is only one—*Halcyornis toliapicus*
from the Eocene of Sheppey, goes back to the Ice Age.

Alcedo atthis is found throughout Eurasia, Northern
Africa, and eastward to the Solomon Islands. It is
widely distributed throughout Britain, except in
northern Scotland where it does not breed. It is at
home on fresh waters of all kinds, and can be found on
the streams of slow-moving rivers, canals, lakes and fen
drains. In autumn there is a partial migration to the
coast among those birds which have no territories and
those whose territories may freeze over. There they
can be found in tidal estuaries, gutters, salt-marshes,
and along rocky sea-shores.

Their main diet is fish, which they catch with lightning speed by diving perpendicularly into the water
and grasping the fish between their mandibles—not, as
some people think, by spearing them. Usually they do

not like to fish in open places, unless there is an extensive amount of fish present. They try to keep to the protective covering of the bankside, perching on an overhanging twig or branch, always at a vantage-point usually three or four feet above the water. When there is no cover or no convenient place to fish from, they can be seen hovering over the water after the manner of a kestrel.

We studied our kingfishers on the River Test in Hampshire. Our home town, Whitchurch, is situated in the north of Hampshire, in a countryside of varied and attractive scenery, ranging from the river valleys of the Test and Bourne to the undulating chalk downs in the north. The climate is congenial with a fair amount of sunshine. Agriculture, barley, wheat, and sheep-farming are still principal industries. Watercress is grown commercially along the Test and Bourne, and Overton has a paper-mill whose traditions go back to Henri de Portal, an 18th-century French Huguenot who gained the Bank of England currency paper contract. Other light industries also operate in the district.

The source of the Test lies east of Overton near the hamlet of Ashe. By the time the stream has flowed only a few miles it has formed itself into a fine strong river. This river is one of the most famous and extensive chalk streams of the country and still remains unspoilt. Here kingfishers are still fairly common and so long as the fishing fraternity exists the waters will never become polluted with industrial effluent, unfortunately so commonplace nowadays. The chalk stream supports trout and, on the lower reaches, salmon.

From Overton the river flows through the beautiful

park at Laverstoke and the wooded hills of Freefolk, to Bere Mill at Whitchurch, where Henri de Portal invented his method of watermarking paper. Below this is where our story begins. The river is wide and beautiful, flowing silently among unspoiled scenery. To set our scene I will describe the river, its fauna and flora.

Beneath the clear water a fine selection of water-weeds in varying shades of green are anchored to the gravelly bed. Between these move the brown trout and the introduced rainbow trout, fine fish weighing several pounds apiece. Also grayling have taken advantage of the amenities, though they are not a true 'game' fish and are frequently removed by electric fishing or when the river is netted. In the mud, eels of considerable length can be found.

The banks of the river are very low and prone to erosion, and so have to be constantly rebuilt. In some places alders are planted and pollarded to make neat hedges and in others they grow prolifically to considerable heights. They are called 'guardian of the meadows' for their matted roots help to bind the crumbling banks against erosion.

The river flows through marshy meadows and grassy valleys. It is framed on either side by picturesque trees. Willows predominate. The weeping willow sweeps its branches across the waterline. A native of China, its slender hanging branches make it a popular ornament of riverside lawns. The leaves of the crack willow change from silver to soft greens in the breeze; the flowers of the pussy willow are some of the first to be visited by the bees and butterflies of spring. There are others. The black poplar shares the love of the willow for moist places. This is regarded as a native tree, unlike the white poplar, or Abele, which rarely exceeds 50 feet in this country. Its leaves move laterally in the wind and their undersides are covered with grey down. The leaves of the black poplar have no down and they rustle in the slightest breeze. Other majestic trees of the riverside are the horse chestnut and sycamore.

On one side of the river, the private side, a wide path is cut by the waterkeeper for the benefit of the many fishermen who frequent the banks from April to September, the fishing season. For the rest of the year the path is seldom used except by the waterkeeper.

On the other side of the river beneath the trees, the bank is lined with thick, dense, and almost impenetrable vegetation. The chief barrier is stinging nettles. Their biting acids make them undesirable to us but they are an all-important foodplant for the caterpillars of the tortoiseshell, red admiral and many other butterflies. Sorrel willow herbs, comfrey, figwort, thistles and parsley choke the grasses or else leave little room for them. The scented creamy flowers of the meadowsweet and the forbidding purple of the deadly nightshade are woven together with the delicate blooms of the greater and lesser bindweed. Brambles, ivy and dogrose bar the way. There is a constant green line of rushes and sedge along the water's edge, where in June the hairy caterpillars of the drinker moth can be heard scrumping leaves on a still night. This moth derives its name from the fact that although the caterpillar feeds on grass it will drink great beads of dew or raindrops. The flags of yellow iris brighten up the water's edge, and later on the scene is enhanced by the flowers of the purple loosestrife. In August and September, the hemp agrimony's pink flowers attract the handsome Red Admiral butterflies. Occasionally we find the beautiful waxy flowers of the bog bean. This marshy jungle is almost impenetrable in high summer, but it makes good cover for the naturalist and his movie camera.

Near the river are the low-lying meadows; many are naturally marshy and some are called water-meadows, for early in the year the hatches from the river are opened to flood these meadows to provide an early supply of grass for the cattle. Here the snipe drum incessantly in their courtship flights and the redshank utters melancholy calls when disturbed. The grass-hopper warbler bursts into reeling song at intervals and the noise is so like the reeling of the line on the fisher-man's rod that it has often deceived me. Its cousin in the sedges chatters incessantly; with a song that is neither musical nor sweet, merely constant, it babbles far into the night, thus earning for its pains the name of 'sedge nightingale.' These little birds are among our first summer visitors. There are other migrants: fly-catchers, warblers, and yellow wagtails. Swallows dip and play about the old corn-mill where some nest, and at night go to roost in the thick blackthorn hedges. High up the swifts reel and scream.

The mallard are an established part of the river, though considered undesirable because they destroy the environment for the trouts' food. In many areas they are now bred in great numbers for 'sportsmen' to shoot. They idle their time away nibbling on the eel grass and sifting through the muds and at night they disappear gradually in the sunset, in small numbers, dropping down into the cornfields where they glean the stubble.

When the waterkeeper cleans off the hatches he leaves a pile of water-weeds, and wagtails, grey and pied, and the resident robin search for aquatic insects and larvae that are stranded in the debris. Coots and moorhen are common, though shy of humans. The distant laughing trill of the dabchick reminds us that we very rarely see it, for at first disturbance it is away, swimming underwater almost as if jet-propelled. Its nest, concealed there, shows no sign of the stained eggs, only an innocent pile of water-weeds floating on the surface.

Early in the morning in the quiet, infrequently fished reaches stands a grey sentinel—the heron, a very shy bird. This rival fisherman is not built for speed like the kingfisher. It will stand motionless in the shallows till an unsuspecting trout or grayling swims past; then, with unerring aim, its head jerks forward and the fish is captured, often stabbed by the upper mandible and held tight against the lower one. The unfortunate fish is carried off to the bank where it is readjusted and swallowed whole.

The mammals, though rarely seen, are still present. Fox and hedgehog prowl about at night. Stoats and rats are numerous along the edge of the cornfield near the river, weasels not so common. Under the piles of rotten vegetation on the river-banks, mice and voles live in their little grassy summer nests, and on the drier banks the high-pitched squeaks of voracious shrews can be heard. The most commonly seen river mammal is the water vole. It is so short-sighted that a quiet observer can watch it at quite close range, swimming to and fro collecting the stems of waterside plants to line its bankside burrows, or on its hind-quarters, munching one of its favourite vegetable foods, the mares-tail, which it eats by holding it between its fore-paws.

Frogs were once fairly numerous in the marshy meadows but now seem to have declined. There are few toads. Sometimes a grass-snake may be found on a bank basking in the sun of a hot summer's day. Newts can sometimes be found in stagnant ditches, and slow-worms on the drier banks.

The surface of the water may seem lifeless but if one watches long enough a trout may rise and take a hatching fly. Soon after another insect may appear and then another, till the whole air is full of them, dancing in myriads over the surface, enough to make an angler's heart rejoice. Mayflies can be seen at the end of May, though not on our particular stretch of river. Their brief life is proverbial; it is the adult winged form that is so short-lived, since before that the nymph, which is entirely aquatic, may have lived as long as three years in its larval form. They feed on minute vegetable matter, like algae and diatoma and fragments of plant tissue. The fully developed nymph floats to the surface. There the case splits and the winged insect emerges—the sub-imago, for the process is not yet complete. This is dull-coloured and called the 'dun.' It flies away to rest among the vegetation. After the final moult has taken place the mayfly is fully coloured and then called the 'spinner.' The dancing flight of the males is rhythmically up and down, and after pairing and once the female has laid her eggs, their short adult life ceases.

The first flies on our part of the river to hatch are the Spring Olives. They are large and smoke-grey, and hatch on cold blustery days. The river may at first seem quite lifeless. Then suddenly the flies begin to appear, for a peculiarity of spring rises is the way they suddenly start and end.

Later, on such days when the wind whips the river into waves it may be difficult to see the flies and even the rises. These are the days of the Iron Blue, which seem to delight in bitter and rough weather and overcast skies. When the Iron Blue is hatching the trout gorge exclusively on them. But the warmer weather of June brings out the pale watery duns and there are evening hatches of sedges. Later, on a warm still evening, Blue-winged Olives may be seen.

Watercress is grown commercially along the Test. The springs that feed the beds where it is grown eventually flow out in streams and into the river. These and the natural streams that flow from the river and back into it farther down are the home of the kingfisher.

Some streams flow parallel to the river and only a few feet from it. These are a quick hiding-place for the moorhen and coot when the waterkeeper or fishermen disturb them. Other streams feed large trout-rearing ponds and, in spring, minnows can be found in the ditches. Other streams are narrow and soon block up with summer vegetation. Although the kingfisher can sometimes be seen hovering over the deeper parts of the river it usually only fishes the shallows that lap the banks. Usually it is seen flying up or down river, on its way from stream to stream where the shallow waters provide it with its main needs. Besides the kingfisher, there is one other elusive bird who lives in the marshy undergrowth—the water rail, which is so secretive and shy that it conceals itself at the slightest disturbance.

The variety of life in these streams is basically the same as that on the river. Small fish are numerous. The water from the river is usually controlled before entering these carriers by an iron hatch. When the river becomes swollen, although the chalk soil quickly soaks away the water after a storm, the hatches are opened to prevent flooding of the banks and the mills, and more water pours into the streams. When the water-level of the river drops as in dry hot summers, the hatches are often closed right up, and often the streams will cease to flow. In the eddying waters under the hatches there are minnows in shoals. The feathery fronds of the water-weeds contain shoals of sticklebacks, and hiding under the large stones on the gravelly bed, the solitary bullhead, a favourite dish of the kingfisher, waits lethargically for night when it can go and hunt unseen by the master fisherman. Other fish less common to the Upper Test are the gudgeon, ten-spined stickleback, brook lamprey and the lobster-like crayfish. Even the gravel is alive, as in the river, with the larvae of the caddis fly. These move slowly across the stones in their horn-shaped shells, which they have built for themselves from pieces of gravel, weed and wood.

This then is the scene where our kingfisher lives. But what of the bird itself, when may it best be seen? The kingfisher is elusive and for the most part quiet. Except in the spring when its noisy courtship proceedings are taking place and in the autumn when the parents are desperately trying to drive away their offspring with angry threats, one might question its very existence. One may explore their whole territory and flush neither of the pair, though they were seen only yesterday, leaving one puzzled by their apparent absence.

Once perched the bird seldom advertises its presence by calling, though its bobbing movements as it watches for fish may betray it. Once disturbed it will disappear in a streak of blue, often before a good view of it can be had. Thereafter it is of no use stalking the bird, for it travels so fast it is soon lost from sight. The only way to see it is to wait in concealment near one of its favourite perches. Any sudden movement, rather than the actual presence of man, worries the bird. The observer is greatly assisted in his search once he has become familiar with the whistle with which the bird usually heralds its approach. As it travels around its territory and always before alighting it sings out once or twice a cheerful high-pitched note '*chee-ee*' probably for the benefit of its mate who might be fishing or resting nearby. Its flight is low except in courtship, usually just above the surface of the water, as swift as an arrow: it has been estimated at well over 45 m.p.h. There is no perceptible slowing down as it approaches a perch. It stops with a jerk; the next second it is sitting quite motionless, quite calm, its head already tilted, watching the water for the next unfortunate fish to betray itself.

Suddenly the ordinary commonplace of the bankside is transformed. The bird is unbelievably brilliant. It was considered in former times that to gaze too long upon its brilliant plumage was harmful to the eyes. But once the bird is in the shade of the trees its bright colours blend well with the surroundings—a paradox perhaps, but in the overhanging vegetation the bird is singularly inconspicuous. However, once seen the kingfisher is unmistakable. Its back is a dazzling cobalt blue or emerald green, depending upon the angle at which the light strikes it. The wings and head are a darker cobalt and the striae glow with rows of azure speckles. Its dumpy tail is cobalt. Underneath it is a warm chestnut orange. It has a white throat or bib and white neck patches. The cheek patches behind the eyes are orange. Its beak is black and dagger-shaped, although the female has an orange or rose-coloured under-mandible, which is the only distinguishing external feature between the sexes. The legs and feet are small and sealing-wax red, and unusual since the second and third toes are joined into one as far as the second joint, a feature peculiar to the species. This dumpy bird is a mere 6½ inches long. Juveniles are slightly duller and smaller than their parents, with shorter black bills and black feet. In older birds the feet colour changes to a deeper red-purple.

Many legends are associated with the kingfisher and all over the world it is connected with the Flood. In the Andaman Islands it is said that the survivors of the Flood were without fire and so, as the spirit of one of the drowned, the bird flew to the gods and stole a burning brand. In the process it burnt its chest. As it turned away a brand fell into the lap of the Creator, who seized it and hurled it after the bird, scorching its rump.

But the most charming legend describing how the kingfisher got its colours originated in France. The peasants of Metz used to tell the following story. While

Noah was waiting for the dove to return to the Ark he turned to the kingfisher, who was then a grey bird, and said: 'You are courageous, or your beak belies you, and you will not fear the waters', and he despatched the little bird to see if the flood had receded. As it flew away a great storm arose and the little bird flew heavenwards to avoid it. It flew so high that the colour of its back was changed to a dazzling blue. Then the sun arose and the kingfisher sped towards it, so scorching the feathers of its breast and underparts. Just in time it turned, but not before its rump was tinged with red. Then it plunged into the water to cool itself. Refreshed and now mindful of its duty, the kingfisher began to search for Noah but was unable to find him, for by then the Ark had been dismantled. Thus the kingfisher obtained its beautiful riot of colours, and to this day the little bird is still searching up and down the riverside for its old master.

In Bohemia the bird was revered as good luck. Others say a single feather is a sure talisman against lightning. Our ancestors ascribed to the Blue One the power of bringing them wealth, peace, and beauty. The kingfisher is often known as 'halcyon.' The word halcyon comes from the Greek ἅλs, the sea, and κυῶν, to brood. Halcyone, the daughter of Aeolus and wife of Ceyx, is said to have learned in a dream that her husband had been drowned in a shipwreck; distraught with grief she threw herself into the sea where his body floated. The gods, impressed with her fidelity, changed both her and her husband into birds—he into a tern or gannet, and she into a kingfisher,[1] birds which haunt

---

[1] Some accounts say they were both changed into kingfishers.

the seashore and mate for life. Further they decreed that when the hen-bird laid her eggs on her floating, seaborne nest, the weather should be fine and calm, whence the tradition of 'halcyon days' seven days before and after the winter solstice, when the kingfisher was said to brood.

2

Early Adventures

FROM 1956, Ron's hobby was cinematography. He
first had a 9.5 mm. camera, but soon came to realise the
limitations of the gauge and graduated to 16 mm. His
first 16 mm. camera was a 1935 Bell and Howell
Filmo. As a part-time projectionist at the local cinema
he was learning what makes a film technically perfect
and, inspired by Walt Disney's nature films, it was not
long before he decided on natural history filming himself.

Around the river there is much life in early spring.
Because of the limitations of his equipment he was
forced to get as close as possible to his subjects. His
longest focal length lens was 75 mm. and because it
was non-reflex, the camera had to be set up on a particular plane with the lens already focused. Birds like
blue-tits could be enticed to feed on crumbs on one
small patch, and rats would forage for corn along a
mossy log which was parallel to the camera. Birds with
their nests, hedge-sparrows, wagtails and wrens, could
be filmed with the use of a hide. Sometimes Ron left
the camera set up near the nest and used remote con-

trol—a piece of thread attached to the push-button of the camera—and in this way got good close-ups of fly-catchers and robins. Most of this filming took place near the river, and the route home passed the water-cress beds. Here the local kingfisher did most of his fishing and on several occasions Ron disturbed it, whereupon it disappeared almost immediately. He tried to stalk it with his camera, but with little result, for the bird proved to be too small in the frame and shot away from the camera in a streak of blue.

During his off-duty period at the cinema he took another job, that of helping the waterkeeper on the river. Here he had the chance of observing the king-fisher on the river, and so his knowledge of its haunts grew. When fishing in a particular area the bird always seemed to sit on the same twig or post. These included the handrail near the waterkeeper's cottage, a stump amongst the blackthorn above the old corn-mill, and the small concrete walls of the cressbeds. There was however one favourite place at the bottom of the cressbeds where a stream from the beds flowed to meet one that came from the river. Here the kingfisher spent a lot more time preening, resting and fishing, probably because the hedges about the stream gave it seclusion. It could stay there all day without being disturbed. Nearby Ron set up a hide, camouflaged with mud and consisting merely of an old blanket on a framework of four broom handles.

Hidden under this makeshift hide, he eventually managed to secure what seemed to be some promising shots of the birds. But with his non-reflex camera there were many difficulties. The kingfisher had to sit upon the exact spot on which the camera was focused.

To make the bird sit closer to the hide, and so to the camera, he placed a better perch than the existing one in a more convenient position, and removed all other likely perching places in the area. Then he noticed that the kingfisher only returned to the perch about once an hour and even then stayed only a few minutes. Presumably there were not enough fish in the area to hold the bird's attention for very long. Perhaps if the number of fish were increased and made fairly visible the bird would be induced to stay longer. It would clearly be pointless just to put fish down into the stream: they had to be kept in one area. A container of some kind was out of the question, for if the bird were frightened away it might never return, a risk Ron could not afford. His answer was to build up part of the stream bed so as to form a little pool.

The bed of the stream was of clean gravel, so he built the pool with gravel walls. When finished, the pool was circular and the wall rose just above the level of the water. While the sediment was settling Ron fetched a flour sieve and a bucket. The sieve was his fishing-net and after exploring one or two of the streams in the cressbeds he soon had enough stickle-backs and bullheads to fill his pool. Once the fish were in the pool they could not get out because the wall was above waterlevel, and some tried to hide by burrowing into the gravel. But there were enough still visible to attract a hungry kingfisher—directly underneath one of its perches. It worked. When the bird came back, it did stay longer, it did take the fish. With this arrangement the kingfisher was assured of a ready meal and thereby became the unsuspecting actor in the film.

But the first film results were disappointing. The kingfisher had been filmed against the light, and the general position was far too much in the shade of the trees. There was nothing for it—hide, perch and pond would have to be moved into the open sunlight.

Although the new pool was about ten yards away from the other one the kingfisher took to the new position with no hesitation at all, and the next reel of film was more promising. The first of the shots were rather distant long ones. The next step was to take close-up shots and so, inch by inch, the hide was moved closer to the perch so that eventually Ron was filming from only three feet away. The kingfisher was completely oblivious of the noise of the camera and took no notice at all of the odd sounds that were issuing from an even odder-looking hide. The kingfisher had a completely black beak, which, although Ron did not realise it at the time, showed that it was a cock bird. So the operation was a success. Ron had captured a kingfisher on film. He turned his attention to other wild life in the vicinity.

It was not until the following spring that he saw the kingfisher again. Out on a walk one evening he saw the bird flying ahead of him in the cressbeds, and next minute heard a commotion. It sounded like the kingfisher calling but was a rather more rapid succession of calls than usual. He crept to the place where he had seen the bird disappear, a narrow stream not far from the one where he had filmed the previous year. The stream was a new one only excavated that winter, as an outlet from some new cressbeds to the river. The banks were about 3 feet high, sheer and, as yet, clear of weeds. From his concealed position behind some very tall butterburr he could see a pair of kingfishers flying in rapid succession at one of the banks of the stream. They were excavating their nesting tunnel. As they were about to concentrate their activities upon nesting, this was obviously a good time to film them again. By dusk he had a hide erected fifteen feet away from the site and the next day he watched them excavating. They took it in turns and often one would fly off and return with a fish for its busy mate. After watching for a while he decided to wait until the young were hatched and two weeks old before he attempted to film them inside the nest. While the birds were excavating they were working in the shadow of the bank and a low film speed of only 10 A.S.A. proved disastrous and resulted in two rolls of under-exposed film. The film that had been taken of the perch, which was more in the sunlight, was correctly exposed and these shots included the courtship feeding, the sequence of the cock feeding the hen with a fish.

A month elapsed before Ron saw any further activity. Occasionally during that time he visited the cressbeds in the hope of seeing the birds, but never once saw them. It was so quiet that he thought they might have deserted, but after five weeks he could just hear the sounds of the youngsters churring like grasshoppers, and he knew that everything was all right.

It was now time to remove the top of the nest. This was a question of simple geometry. By Ron's calculations the nest chamber lay directly beneath a large turf of grass. By carefully removing this and a little more of the earth he was able to detach the ceiling of the chamber and find the hidden youngsters. There were six of them and they were all clothed in quills, or spiky jackets. The nest was simply a depression in the earth surrounded by fragments of fishbones. It was quite clean, for all the excreta was in the tunnel. This eventually looked like a white marble corridor, and it was from this that the rather unpleasant strong fishy smell drifted up.

No attempt was made to film the young that day. The nest was covered up with plywood and stones as protection against night predators. He left them till next day, planning to return and film them in open sunlight if the weather permitted.

It took just half an hour next morning to set a second hide behind the nest, after which Ron retreated to the observation hide on the opposite bank to make sure that the parents were accepting their modified home and the new hide which was so close to the nest. But the kingfishers went on, in and out of the nest, each with one fish at a time, completely undisturbed by their new ceiling. As there was nothing to fear, Ron began slowly to uncover the nest. He pulled back the plywood inch by inch over a period of two hours. The day was clear and warm and the sunlight soon flooded the little birds, who had previously seen so little in the dim light that reached them from two feet of tunnel. Although the parents had been going in and out as the light in their nesting chamber increased, it was still a breathtaking moment when one eventually entered the tunnel and found its young bathed in full sunlight. But the bird was not harassed or upset and went on feeding casually and normally. The fish was presented head first to the youngster nearest the tunnel entrance and it was fed whole, not, as some think, torn up and shared out amongst the youngsters. After feeding, the parent backed down the hole even though it could have left via the top. Clearly it did not associate the lighting of its home and the hole in the ceiling with a way of entering and leaving the nest. The food the parents brought to the nest consisted of minnows, sticklebacks and bullheads.

Ron attached little interest to the shots of the birds feeding in the nest as he thought that this must have already been filmed. The sequence of the courtship feeding and the shots of the kingfisher fishing, together with the new ones of the young being fed, made a pleasant sequence for his film on the River Test. The finished film, which included many well-known scenes of the river, as well as of the fauna and flora, became quite popular with local audiences. Eventually the film was shown at a meeting of the Nature Cine Club in London, and as a result the series producer of I.T.V.'s 'Survival' programme was told of the kingfisher sequence and became interested in it. On viewing the film, though, it was decided that the sequence could not be used on television for two technical reasons. The film stock was unsuitable for the television system and the film had been shot at 16 frames per second instead of 25 frames per second at which speed the television system transmits it.

Now the ultimate decision was to reshoot the kingfisher sequence at the correct speed on a newer and faster film stock. I too had been interested in birds as a result of some English lessons with a local ornithologist. We spent much more time watching birds from his study windows than we should have on those

Saturday mornings, and my interest in birds grew and continued throughout my latter schooldays.

When I first met Ron he was about to reshoot the kingfisher sequence on the new film stock, Kodachrome II, and I was delighted to help him with his project. I was more than amazed to find such a beautiful small bird so close to our homes yet so rarely seen and relatively unknown. It was in 1962 that we located the kingfishers again. This time it was on a different part of the river behind the old corn mill. They were making a feeble attempt at excavating the stony banks of a small trout-rearing pond near the mill. One day the activity came to an abrupt end when a neighbour's cat brought one of the kingfishers home dead. We had lost our opportunity to film the pair for the year, so we began to search the Test high and low visiting all the places where people told us kingfishers used to nest.

We searched all the banks and the streams of the river that were high enough to nest in. We searched overgrown chalk pits and banks that had been made by the roots of uprooted trees, and in early summer concluded that we were too late to find a nest. And so we abandoned the project for the year.

The following year we shot some of the film sequences we needed and took them back to the 'Survival' producer. When he saw the film he decided there was no survival theme to relate the sequence to his programme and referred us to the B.B.C. Natural History Unit at Bristol who made among other programmes 'Look', to which the material might be more suited. Late that year the film was viewed by them, and the material was used as a short item on one of their programmes since at that stage there was not enough film

for a 'Look' programme. We then discovered that the
kingfisher had rarely been successfully photographed
and that a film study on the birds' life might be a 'first.'
It was decided to make a 25-minute 'Look' programme
on the kingfisher on yet another type of colour film,
for now we all had colour television in mind.

3

A Stream for the Fish

It HAD BECOME quite obvious to us that if we were to make a film on kingfishers we must do it with one pair of birds in their own territory. We knew that they were territorial and that the cock and hen in the breeding season shared a territory, but the problem was in finding a pair. There was one pair of kingfishers that again haunted the local cressbeds and the other streams above the old corn-mill. A kingfisher was seen, too, below the old corn mill, at a stream which fed through the marshy field, through the trout-rearing pond where last year's ill-fated pair had attempted to dig, and then back out into the main river again. This marshy field was private and quiet, unlike the cressbeds which by day were frequented by the cressbed workers and in the evening by the local children fishing for tiddlers. Few people ever disturbed the tranquillity of the marsh; usually it was only a case of the waterkeeper on his way from his cottage downstream to his beat upstream. In the summertime the fishermen sometimes fished nearby, but by and large they spent more time upon the water above the old mill.

Mac, the waterkeeper, told us that he often saw a

kingfisher in the early morning at the junction of the trout-rearing pond and the outlet stream. Whether or not the pair from the cressbeds owned this stream he was unable to say, but we soon discovered that they did.

We went with him and examined the stream. There seemed to be no fish visible there but we thought that could quickly be changed. The great thing was to be able to work with the birds on a private piece of land—which is very necessary for nature filming, since birds and animals are so easily disturbed by the public at large. Our idea was to have a stream that we could permanently stock with a generous amount of fish, so that the kingfisher, we hoped, would spend most of his time there, in preference to the more difficult meals he was used to.

Mac gave us permission to use the stream. It would not disturb his work, as the trout-rearing pond was not in use yet. The outlet stream was about 12 feet long and he suggested that we build grids at either end to keep in our stock of fish. Fish could be acquired with a little cunning from any of the streams of the river or the cressbeds.

We set to work that very morning, clearing the stream of weeds, sticks, stones, mud, and dead vegetation. As it was to be a film set, we had to endeavour to make it as pretty as possible and it had to be prepared well ahead of time. We planted reeds and ferns on the bank for colour. Once all the mud in the stream had been washed away by the current we were left with a gravelly bed, and then we put in the grids, first the one at the top and then the other at the outlet of the stream. The reasons for not wanting any mud in the stream, besides its basic unsightliness, were that the fish would

37

hide in it and that, more important, the lighter the colour of the gravelly river-bed, the more light it would reflect up on to the bird, an asset when working with a colour film of low light sensitivity.

The grids were made of wire gauze fixed to wooden posts, and we thought them substantial enough until the first storm only three days later, when the swollen waters swept away the wire gauze and all the fish with it. After this misfortune we used proper heavy iron rods and hammered them into the bed of the stream, attaching the new gauze to the front of them. This new gauze had a finer, stronger mesh, which was still big enough to let the water flow freely. It would have to be cleaned off daily to prevent the green algae and floating aquatic vegetation from clogging the mesh. This job would be done in the evenings after work on our visits to the stream to replenish the fish supply.

By the time we had got home from work those early February evenings there was only a short time left to go fishing and it was often dark before we had located the fish. The most locally common fish were sticklebacks, the cressbeds abounding in them. There were minnows, too, in other streams and ponds, and bullheads could be found, though singly, in both places. These three types of fish we thought would constitute the kingfisher's diet.

The stickleback, the three-spined variety, we found in gutters in the cressbeds. In the early part of the year catching them was exceptionally easy, for they could be found torpid in the mud. Armed with a large dredging-net nearly as wide as the gutters themselves, we paddled up dredging through the mud; but the warmer weather brought the sticklebacks out and one of us then had to walk downstream driving the shoal before us into the waiting net. In this manner we were able to catch a fair amount for our kingfisher 'bird table.' Sticklebacks are called by most of us tiddlers, tittlebacks, redthroat, or prickleback. They gain the name three-spined from the fact that the spiny rays of the first part of the dorsal fin are separate and usually number three. Along the lateral line towards the tail there are a few large scutes or plate-like scales. These fish are principally found in freshwater streams and ponds. When the male assumes his breeding colours he is especially handsome. The silver belly changes to scarlet and the upper parts shine with a fluorescent green. It is he that establishes the nest into which he entices as many females as he can. When the eggs are laid and fertilised he mounts guard, driving away all intruders including the mothers. This unusual behaviour makes him the only British freshwater fish not only to build the nest but to guard it too.

Minnows are much bigger and, we thought, would be much harder to catch. They belong to the same family as the goldfish, tench, and carp, and grow to a maximum of 3½ inches. The winter quarters of these fish are the deeper parts of the river, ponds and streams, places we often could not reach with our dredging-net. We therefore had to find a different way of catching them. Traps were the answer. It is an old fisherman's method of catching minnows for bait. We baited large sweet jars with bread and then sank them into the water, where we had seen minnows present. The lids of the jars were replaced with conical gauze funnels. The unsuspecting fish would find their way into the jars easily enough, guided by the funnel, but after feeding on the bread would be very lucky to find the small hole which led back to freedom again. We often pulled up those jars the next day to find them full of minnows. But as the last of the wintery days passed, the bread in the jars remained untouched. At first we thought the fish were escaping. But the traps in other areas showed the same negative result. Then we realised. The minnows had gone upstream to spawn and had moved out into the shallow streams. Sure enough we found them surging behind the hatches in their hundreds. We were lucky enough to catch twenty or thirty of them in our dredging-net at one go.

It was catching the bullheads that took most of our time. As they are a solitary fish they can only be caught one at a time. This ugly fish has an oversize head and a most excellent system of camouflage. They can adapt themselves perfectly to match the colours of their surroundings, from a uniform colour in mud to a varied one in gravel, and on a gravelly bed they are scarcely distinguishable from the stones. In these waters they grow to about $3\frac{1}{2}$ inches, though the kingfisher would never take them that big. The bullhead has an unpleasant family background for it is related to the scorpion fish of the British coastlines. Fortunately though, it lacks the venom of its relatives and any wounds inflicted by its spiny fins are innocuous. It hides by day under large stones but at night goes out in search of larvae and aquatic insects, freshwater shrimp, worms, and fish eggs and fry. For the latter it is disliked by riparian owners and bailiffs. We were never able to find many of these fish in the main river, for they were always in the carriers and ditches. The method we used for catching them was to walk upstream lifting up the stones of the river bed with one hand and having the other hand ready in the water to grab the fish from behind. During the day they are so sleepy that this proves quite easy, the only disadvantage being the coldness of the water on a wintry day.

And so our stream soon became stocked with fish. The water was only a few inches deep, easy fish offered for easy catching. A perch was placed over the stream midway between the two grids, but at first nothing happened. Then the fish began to disappear, too rapidly for a kingfisher to have been responsible. We approached the stream under cover of the bushes and discovered a moorhen standing in our 'table' eating the fish. This we soon remedied. We raised the water-level in the stream so that the bird would have to dive for the kingfisher's fish. Whether or not this made any difference I am not sure, but the moorhen did not come back.

We were not able to watch at the stream by day but one evening the waterkeeper told us that he had seen a kingfisher at the stream for three consecutive mornings, and later we found that the obliging bird had left its sloshy white visiting card under the perch, which showed at least that he must be a fairly regular visitor. Encouraged by this, we began to build our first hide, one week after preparing the stream. Twelve feet away from the perch we erected a wooden framework, with the four corner-posts driven hard into the ground, and over this we laid a canvas cover. As canvas hides often flap in the wind and disturb the bird we thatched the walls with dead vegetation so that they were eventually 6 inches thick. These matched well with the surrounding area but thatching proved a mistake, for after two months of very wet weather the thatch began to rot and the rain dripped down our necks as we tried to film. The fact that the hide was immovable also meant that we had to build other hides when we wanted a change of camera angle. Eventually we invested in some hardboard and roofing-felt and made a movable box hide, 4 ft. × 4 ft. × 4 ft. This we could roll up and down the banks of the stream or pond, or even across the stream to the other side; at one time we hung it on iron rails over the stream. Camouflage we did not bother with for even before we had finished building the hide we found that the kingfisher was using it as a perch.

4

The Kingfisher's Diet

OUR HIDE was accepted by the birds as being nothing out of the ordinary, and the stream became a regular part of the cressbed kingfisher's territory. After spending some time at the stream the visiting kingfisher would fly back in the direction of the cressbeds. Every evening we were busy catching fish and as the days grew longer there was enough time left to watch the kingfisher and sometimes its mate fishing.

As we watched and began to learn the different techniques they used to kill the different types of fish, we began to plan the best places and angles from which to film them. This meant, of course, that the position of the perch would have to be changed so that the kingfisher would appear to be fishing in a different part of the river. This constant exchanging of perches, sometimes as often as three times a day, did not upset the kingfisher. It always expected to find a perch there and did not seem to mind what type it was or in what part of the stream it was placed. (Usually it was placed near the centre, depending on whether we were taking a long shot, mid-shot or close-up.) It was, though,

43

completely baffled if the perch was taken away altogether. It would hover over the area momentarily
where the last perch had been placed, and then retreat
either to the top of the hide or to one of the grids.
When the grids were uncovered the kingfisher spent a
long time on them rather than on the perches. Most of
the time, however, the grids were covered up and we
tied bunches of grass and weeds to the top of them to
make them feel unsteady as perches. The kingfisher
will perch on nothing that feels unfirm.

In late March, 1963, we were still using a non-reflex
camera. This, if perfectly set up with the bird sitting
in exactly the right place, produced good enough
results. But we realised that a reflex camera would be
more of an asset and eventually exchanged our Bell and
Howell for a reflex Bolex.

Before arriving on the set the kingfisher always
called. In this way it usually woke us up, for the long
wait in a darkened hide would make us drowsy. On
landing it would sit quite still, head on one side watching for any movement in the water. Occasionally it
jerked its head to one side. Even with a large number
of fish in the stream it was often some time before the
bird lined up on a good-sized one. Sometimes it would
fluff out all its feathers and relax, though apparently it
still watched the water closely, for it would often
become instantly alert again. On sighting its quarry it
would tense itself, bring all its feathers close to its
body, and then—quick as lightning—it was gone. A
split second after plunging headlong into the water it
was back on the log with a fish in its beak. Here the
log came into its own. Had the perch been a springy
one, like some of the branches which overhang the

water, the bird might have taken the fish away to a more substantial perch to kill it. As it was, a quick slap against the side of the log and the minnow was swallowed headfirst.

To film this sequence we had used a mossy log placed mid-stream. Of course the camera did not show it as such. On the film the kingfisher appeared to sit on part of a mossy log looking down into the water. By starting the camera up when the bird sighted its quarry and tensed itself for the dive, we were able to show it on the log, leaving the log, returning to it, and killing and eating the fish, all in one shot. But it was the gap between the bird leaving the perch and returning to it that needed to be filled in. The whole action of the bird actually catching the fish was far too fast to be seen clearly and we began to ponder devious means by which we might film it.

Meanwhile we went on to film the kingfisher catching a bullhead. Normally this fish lies under the big stones of the gravelly river-bed. One stream that flows above the mill is fairly fast and deep in places. The cressbed kingfisher would spend a lot of time in the bushes about this stream when the men were working in the cressbeds. The birds sat at positions six to eight feet higher than they did when working the cressbeds, when they fished contentedly from the 10-inch high walls. It could be that it is easier to work a fast stream from higher up, and slow-running water from lower down. In both places there were perches of varying heights.

This stream was nevertheless full of bullheads, and we caught a good number to take back to our stream. We borrowed a tin bath from the waterkeeper and put

the bullheads in it, anchoring it to the bank of the
stream. A new log replaced the old mossy one, to give
a change of scenery. When the kingfisher caught the
bullhead it was treated in quite a different way from
that of the minnow. The bird clasped the fish tightly
just above the tail. A fish so big and bulky required a
good deal of effort. It was swung by the tail time and
time again, against the log, its poor head coming
down with dull thuds until it was stunned or, if its head
was too big, pulverised. With its fins flattened to its
sides, it was then swallowed head first; unless the fins
are completely flat the bird might choke. A bird as big
as a moorhen has been known to choke on a bullhead,
when swallowing it tailfirst and probably not dead
either. When this happens the fins are pushed open
in the throat and the fish becomes lodged there, so
causing the untimely death of the bird.

Whereas the kingfisher would waste no time killing
a minnow, the stickleback was quite a different problem. The spines of its back and sides must be flattened.
Juvenile kingfishers try to swallow these fish as if they
were minnows, only to regurgitate them with their
spines still erect. They have to beat them hard against
the perch many more times, and the spines only flatten
once the fish is quite dead.

These were the three types of fish the kingfisher was
taking from our stream. While we were getting some
film the kingfisher was getting the best hand-picked
fish. At various periods during the two years we were
filming the kingfishers, we had chances to try out various other food types.

At a loss what to film the kingfisher doing one sunny
afternoon, we dug up some worms behind the set. We

took some time to find enough for they were a couple of feet below the topsoil. When we had enough sizable ones we placed them in a tin bath and awaited the result. We did not really expect the kingfisher to take worms when there were so many fish available to it, and, indeed, it did not.

We had been on the look-out for some time for newts, and when a local keeper told us that a disused swimming-pool full of newts was being broken up and that once most of the water was out they would be very easy to catch, we were soon on the scene with bucket and net. They proved to be the smooth variety and we caught about sixty of them. Back at the stream some went into the tin bath. We retreated into the hide thinking that the kingfisher could not possibly resist such a dish. But it could. After peering at them for several minutes it caught a minnow instead and flew off. We took the newts and released them in various ditches and ponds around the marshy meadow.

By far the oddest of these fishing adventures concerned elvers. The old corn mill stands astride the river and the water flows through the two culverts fast and furious, where fifty years ago it used to turn the grinding mills for the miller. There is no other way for the water, either through or around.

One day the waterkeeper told us that the elvers were swarming upstream and when they reached the mill they were 'stuck,' unable to get through the strong current. But their urge to get upstream was so strong that, defeated in the attempt to get through the mill waters, they tried to climb up the mill wall. This was very hard to believe until we saw the evidence. Above the right-hand culvert there were elvers of various lengths up to nine or ten inches, at different heights on the wet wall of the mill, slithering slowly upwards.

The splash-back from the culvert kept the wall damp for about 4 feet, at which level there was one elver struggling. When it reached the dry bricks it lost its grip and fell back into the seething water below. We found the place from which the elvers were starting off —a tiny gully to one side where the water was virtually still. They slid up the wet bricks and through the ivy which covered the lower part of the wall, then they were back on the wet bricks. The whole process of getting up the wall took several hours and this surge went on for two or three days before it ceased. After we had filmed this for the record, we caught some of the smaller elvers for the kingfisher to try.

Once they were in the tin bath we watched intently to see what the kingfisher's reaction would be, and on arrival its attention was immediately arrested by these tasty morsels and for some time it watched them closely. Then it dived down and caught one and returned to the log with it. It was a bit undecided what to do next for the eel was wriggling hard, wrapping itself around the kingfisher's head and the bird was doing its best to hold on to it. It was holding it tightly enough till it tried to swing it against the perch; then it must have loosened its grip, for the eel fell out. It was four or five inches long, and the kingfisher never tried for another.

Once we found a brook lamprey in the kingfisher's nest. We wondered if the birds ate many of these and sought to obtain some alive. We thought we might be able to electric-fish them out of ditches, but we were wrong. We rigged up a 220-volt generator, worked by a two-stroke engine. We put two D.C. electrodes

THE UNDERWATER DIVE

Left, straight as an arrow the kingfisher plunges towards the bullhead, beak open, eyes closed. *Right*, as soon as the catch is made the bird prepares to flap its way back to the surface

Left, holding its trophy aloft the bird is poised to leave the water on the downstroke of its wings, like a rocket leaving its launching-pad, *right*. Total time for the complete underwater sequence: a third of a second

The aggressive display of a male kingfisher, wary of a territorial intruder: upright stance with wings drooping and bill pointing menacingly

The cock, finally enraged, launches its attack on the stuffed kingfisher (*p.* 121)

in the water and produced not one lamprey. We tried again at a likely looking lamprey ditch but with no result, and we gave up hope of ever catching any of these creatures. But one day whilst fishing for minnows in a muddy ditch near home I caught a brook lamprey instead. Lamprey pie was once an important feature of state banquets, though it is said to be indigestible and Henry the First is reputed to have died of a surfeit of them. Whether it used to have the same effect on the kingfisher or not I do not know. Certainly our birds ignored the lamprey.

Tadpoles too were viewed with disdain. But I once saw our kingfisher take the larvae of a caddis-fly, although it ignored them in bulk. We tried to find a crayfish small enough for them but without success. (The courtship feeding of a pair of kingfishers was once observed in which the crayfish acted as the gift, though the female had some difficulty in swallowing it.) Crayfish do not exist as far upstream as Whitchurch; it is said locally that they stop with the salmon and the mayfly at Longparish. One can therefore safely assume that the kingfishers on the upper Test have never seen crayfish.

It has been reported that the kingfisher will take insects. At Eye Brook Reservoir in Leicestershire, a kingfisher was seen hovering over a small area of long grass, rushes and sedge. Any alert naturalist would consider the sight of a fish-eating bird hovering over grass unusual. It turned out, in fact, that the bird was hawking insects after the manner of a spotted flycatcher.

In Spain the kingfisher, although feeding normally on small fish, also hovers regularly over reed beds picking off the dragonflies that have settled there. Mr. J. T. R. Sharrock the observer of this also saw a kingfisher hovering over the sand dunes, and he thought that it could only be watching for the large spiders to emerge from their burrows there.

One kingfisher was reported to be a rogue. It had been successfully fishing from a height of 14 feet when it suddenly dropped to a perch some eleven feet below. A dipper was coming ashore with a beakful of food, just under the kingfisher's perch. Just as it was about to eat the fish the kingfisher dropped down on it and after a scuffle the dipper retreated and left the kingfisher with the fish. This happened three times altogether, after which the dipper went off and the kingfisher went farther downstream.

It would seem that the kingfisher takes advantage of the largest amount of one or more food types in its area, leaving other food types till they are really needed. Fish are its main diet on rivers, lakes and reservoirs, but those birds living near the coast seem to eat mostly shrimps and molluscs. On average it will make a catch every two or three dives, but a juvenile may dive eight or ten times before making a successful one. An adult may not necessarily miss just because it reappears with no fish. Often it dives in merely to disturb the fish in the water, or to make sure that there are some present.

5

Filming the Kingfisher Under Water

THE STREAM was fine for taking shots of the kingfisher fishing in wide angle, and we were able to take some good ones of the bird killing and eating the various fish on logs and branches, and afterwards shaking itself as if to settle the fish. As yet, though, we had nothing on film of the bird's actions between leaving and returning to the perch. It was essential at least to show the bird hitting the water. For this shot the camera would have to be trained on a particular spot, approximately $1\frac{1}{2}$ square feet of water. The way the stream was set at that time, there was no means of anticipating where the kingfisher would next choose to make its plunge. Fish were swimming up and down the whole 12-foot length of the stream. Minnows surged to the topmost grid, the sticklebacks tried to hide in the shallow patch of accumulated mud and the bullheads were either camouflaged like the gravel or had burrowed under the bank. Nevertheless the kingfisher always knew where they were.

Now we had to limit the kingfisher's diving to only one place. The aim was to concentrate all the fish in one area. A gravelly pool was all right for a few hours but after that, as Ron discovered a year or two before, the current soon washed away the walls. The fish would have to be put in a container of some kind. The tin bath was ruled out, for it would show through the water for what it was. Finding a container of the right specifications was difficult. It had to be 1 ft. 6 ins. wide and about 6 to 8 ins. deep, and it had to match with the rest of the stream.

Eventually we found the answer. A purloined dust-bin lid turned upside-down with very fine gravel cemented inside, placed on the bed of the stream and balanced by large stones, matched well and from above looked just like part of the stream. When the lime in the cement had washed away about two days later, we laid in it the most tempting bullheads we could find. These fish were chosen because they would, once settled, lie quietly on the bottom of the 'pool.' They could not burrow into the stones, for there were none. (Except when fish were in short supply, we put large stones over them so that the kingfisher could not take them whilst we were at lunch.) The lid was positioned so that the rim was just above the water-level. As the fish did not attempt to escape we sank it lower, below the level of the water, which was better from the film-ing point of view. As for the rest of the stream we did not want the bird's attention to wander, for the film which we were buying was costly, and if the kingfisher dived from the perch and did not go into the pool and we had pressed the button thinking it had, we would be wasting film, money, fish, time and precious sunlight (if any). The easiest way to deal with the rest of the fish in the stream was to get them under cover. We dragged some large stones from the main river and put them into the stream. These stones were covered with a surplus of waterweeds, and the fish, several hundred of them, soon disappeared like magic beneath them.

When the kingfisher arrived it spent about ten minutes looking at the fish, as if undecided which to choose. Probably it had never seen so many bullheads before in one part of a stream. We waited for it to fish but it made no attempt. This was disappointing because the sun was right and the fish and the bird were ready and waiting. Still the kingfisher sat fluffed out. What could be wrong? Suddenly it alerted itself then started to retch. We watched in amazement as at the third gulp it brought up a pellet. Of course we knew about pellets for we often found them on top of the hide, but never before had the kingfisher ejected one in front of us. Unfortunately we were unable to film it, as the camera was focused on the water where we hoped the bird would dive into frame. The pellet dropped into the water and disintegrated immediately. It was made of the clean fishbones and spines of the bird's last meal, and usually it has to be ejected before the bird can eat more fish. Once rid of this it began to take an interest in the pool again. Already lined up on a fish it tensed itself and as we pressed the button, so it dived, and for the first time ever we captured it on film hitting the water and emerging with a fish. But the action was hardly revealing at 24 f.p.s. and as the sunlight grew stronger we were able to adjust the camera to run the film through faster at 64 f.p.s. so that we could slow the action down on projection.

Then we became more ambitious. We had seen the bird leave the perch, hit the water, and emerge with a fish. But what of the bird when it was actually in the water, and how could we film this? It would *have* to be filmed somehow for a film-study of a fish-eating bird would be of little value if it did not actually show the bird in the act of seizing its prey. There were two alternatives—to film it naturally or to film it unnaturally. It would be almost impossible to do it naturally for the camera would have to be set up under the water, and then there could be no guarantee that the bird would take the fish near the camera. Even if this were possible there would be insufficient light under the water.

We could film it unnaturally as long as we did not hurt the birds in any way or make them appear to be doing something they did not normally do. The demand for good lighting conditions topped the list as the action would have to be filmed at 64 f.p.s. The only way to achieve this would be to induce the king-fisher to dive into a container simulated to look like a cross-section of the river-bed—like the dustbin lid, only much deeper—for the longer the bird was in the water and the deeper it had to dive the better.

We constructed our first piece of underwater apparatus. It was a disused enamel lightshade about a foot deep and we stood it on a tin box in the stream. The camera looked up at the fish through a perspex porthole to the side and near the bottom. We cemented gravel to the inside in the same manner as we had to the dustbin lid, and then loose gravel was arranged so that the fish were as near as possible to the porthole. The whole thing was such a spectacle that it was a wonder the kingfisher ever accepted it, let alone dived into it. But it did; not at first, for it was a little disturbed and the eyeline was wrong. The perch over it was far too much to the side of the dish. The bird could see that there was something amiss between the water-level in the pool and the water-level of the stream (some 4 feet separated the two), but it seemed excited at seeing the fish there, craning its neck and moving down the perch.

When it flew off without catching anything we immediately re-positioned the perch, this time directly above the dish. Some half an hour later on its next trip round its territory, the kingfisher landed on his perch and this time could see no difference in water-levels, only water surrounded by water. But there was still one more problem to solve. We had never before used the camera on the kingfisher out of the hide. Whilst the camera was in the hide the splashing of the water at the grids drowned its clockwork noise. Now the camera was close to the bird. A cable release led from the camera into the hide and as the kingfisher began to dive we pressed the tip. The bird was about mid-way between the perch and the pool when it must have heard the camera noise. Its immediate reaction was to stop in mid-air, then return to the perch. Its reactions must be really like lightning. The unfamiliar noise of the camera had upset it; of course we should have run the camera first with no film in it till the bird became used to the noise. There was no time for this now. The only thing to do was to run the camera again, which we did, and the kingfisher sat on the perch and listened, cock-ing his head curiously to the unfamiliar noise. Then the camera ran down, as clockwork eventually does, and since it could only be rewound in the kingfisher's absence we had to wait.

When the bird flew off, we slipped out of the hide and rewound the camera, tying our pullovers round it to help deaden the noise. Soon the kingfisher returned, obviously intent on getting the fish. After viewing them interestedly it jumped into the ten inches of water in the dish, and emerged triumphantly. We filmed this at 24 f.p.s., 48 f.p.s. and 64 f.p.s. Each time only one shot could be obtained per kingfisher visit, but after several days we thought at least one of the shots must have been successful, so we anxiously awaited the films' return from the processing laboratory. When we saw the result we were amazed, for the entire fishing sequence at 24 f.p.s constituted only five frames of film, and about eleven at 64 f.p.s. We knew then that it was useless to capture such a sequence on an ordinary camera. What was really needed was a high-speed one.

When the B.B.C. Natural History Unit had become interested in the film they understood what a unique sequence could be achieved. Early the following year, 1964, we recorded this sequence at 300 frames per second.

To film underwater properly we needed an aquarium. We made one 2 ft. long and 1½ ft. wide and deep, with a perspex front and sides made of wood. We loaded it with fish and placed it in the stream. At first the water-level inside was only 4 ins. deep, but we increased it daily until the kingfisher and its mate were diving into water 14 ins. deep. They came to love the aquarium, using it as a perch and shuffling fast round the sides, peering in. But when we were filming we had to keep them off the sides and to do this we placed foam rubber strips round the edges, much to their disgust.

By filming the kingfishers diving into 14 ins. of water at 300 f.p.s., we reckoned on slowing the action down enough to see what the bird was doing. To use the high-speed camera a three-phase electricity supply had to be laid on. This supply was useful for it meant we could use artificial light to supplement the February daylight. The kingfishers behaved well in front of the new camera and in the afternoons, as dusk was approaching, they still remained catching fish under the spotlights.

Normally the kingfisher will not fish in 14 ins. of water, and even when fishing a lake the bird will wait for the fish to surface. But these birds had adapted themselves to the aquarium and seemed to enjoy catching the bullheads in it. By diving directly from the perch into the aquarium, they ended up just short of the bottom. To reach the fish they had to fly upwards a few feet first to get enough impetus and then drop into the water.

The film results showed that the kingfisher closed its wings before entering the water and, once in, plunged straight towards the fish with its beak open, grasping it between the mandibles. Using the buoyancy of its own body and wings, it then flapped its way back to the surface, leaving the water on the downstroke of its wings. The whole action took about a third of a second. If it missed the fish it usually took the nearest thing to it, a stone, which it dropped before emerging.

The most exciting part of the proceedings was not revealed on the cine film, where the resolution was very bad. Two years later we reshot the sequence on a 35 mm. still camera, and some of the clearer shots revealed something quite fantastic. Whilst the kingfisher was in the water its eyes were closed and the nictating membrane, which showed as an opaque blue on the film, was pulled tightly across its eyes. What a feat, to catch a fish blindfolded!

The only other method the kingfisher has of catching its fish is by hovering. This it does when there is a good supply of fish and no convenient perch, and when forced to fish on places such as open estuaries and sea shores. In these instances the kingfisher appears as a blue haze, a small bird hovering over a patch of reeds and pools in the estuary. It hovers kestrel-like in the air for several seconds, some four or five feet above water-level. If it sees a morsel, a small mollusc or crustacean, it will dive, make its catch, and retreat into the reed patch to eat it. After some time it will reappear and start hovering again. If it sees nothing it will drop back into the grass—the only instance I have ever seen of a kingfisher on the ground.

Our own birds seldom hovered. For filming purposes, we tried to make them do so by taking away their perches, whereupon they sat on the hide, and by sinking the tin bath containing the fish in the pond above the stream. The hen bird found the fish lying directly in her flight line from the cressbeds to the stream. (This shows what marvellous eyesight a kingfisher has, for she only flew past them once.) Then she retreated to the tree at the bottom of the pond. She spent ten minutes or so flying backwards and forwards across the pond from the tree to one diagonally opposite it. On the seventh journey she plunged, from a considerable height, headlong into the bath and emerged with a fish. She had no intention of hovering and had outwitted us with her cunning. We did not try again.

6

A Place to Nest

Many legends are associated with the nest and nesting place of the kingfisher. The ancients said that it was a light and fragile structure built upon the seashore (though others state it was built on the sea) which, when finished, was launched upon the waves. In either case the structure was of very frail materials, such as fishbones, which would shatter at the slightest swell. Because of this it was thought that whilst the kingfisher was incubating, seven days before and seven days after the winter solstice, there was a period of perfect calm known as halcyon days.

Despite the ancient legends the real nest is found in an unusual place—a hole in a sheer bank leads through a tunnel to a circular chamber. Some people have thought that the birds take over the holes of the water vole, but this is unlikely. Most usually the tunnel of the chamber is excavated by the pair in a bank of a river or stream in their territory. Normally the kingfisher on our part of the Test keeps well away from those banks which the water vole has undermined. All nest holes in the river or stream banks have to be well above high-water mark, otherwise disaster will result when the river floods. Some rivers do not have high enough banks (even the banks of the Test are very low), and the birds will then have to resort to other sites. The nest may be found in a sand pit, or sometimes in the topmost layer, the clay, of a chalk or gravel pit. Another uncommon place on the Test is a rather unusual 'bank.' After storms, when the banks are flooded, large willow trees and alders can be found uprooted along the side of the river. Among these roots in the depths of the fine loamy soil the kingfisher will often burrow out a hole, and such sites are often used for many years. Sometimes the banks of lanes are used, and on the Isle of Wight the birds have been reported nesting in clefts of caves. Often when there is no site on the river they will nest in holes of stone walls or bridges. One nest in Holland was found in a rabbit hole, because there were no other sites available, and one British pair of kingfishers used the same nest in a bank for so many years that eventually the entrance attained the size of a rabbit hole. If the nest has been made in a solid bank it may be used for many years running and the pair will do nothing more than clear it out at the beginning of each new nesting season.

Once the pair have selected their nesting site they will attack various points of the bank, driving in their bills to loosen the soil. When a reasonable depression appears they concentrate on that spot until they make a foothold or unearth a root to cling to. Then, clutching on to the bank, they will peck away the soil after the manner of a woodpecker until eventually they can sit in the entrance and do the same. Both birds take it in turns to dig, one resting while the other one is working. Once they can sit in the first few inches of the tunnel the real work begins. They dig inwards, making a tunnel that rises slightly upwards. The length of the tunnel depends mainly upon the pliability of the soil. The shortest one on record is 9 inches, the longest 4½ feet. The former was excavated in hard clay, the latter in sand. The tunnel rises slightly upwards, probably to let, later on, the liquid excrement of the young out.

At the end of the tunnel the birds make a chamber which is almost spherical. There is a depression in the floor for the eggs to be laid in. Sometimes, when the tunnel rises at too great an angle and the depression is too slight (this may occur in hard soils), the kingfisher may lose some of its eggs. One pair of kingfishers lost their whole clutch when they left the nest and the eggs rolled out behind them.

The eggs number from five to seven, and, like most white eggs, have the appearance of being pink when first laid. They are deposited on the bare earth of the chamber, and eventually rejected pellets thrown up by the hen during laying and by both birds during incubation accumulate around them. The eggs are *not* laid on fishbones, as some maintain, for if they did, why would the birds bother to clean out old nests? They could go straight in and start laying the eggs on the fishbones already there, whereas in fact they spend two, sometimes three days removing all the fishbones until the floor of the chamber is back to fine bare earth. There is only one exception to the rule. Where the birds have nested continually year after year in the same hole the 'cup' of fishbones hardens, sometimes to such an extent that the birds cannot get it out. On occasions the 'cup' has been found to be crawling with maggots at the end of the breeding season—though this is certainly exceptional. It is this cup-shaped accumulation that was assumed to be the nesting material of the kingfisher. Usually at the end of the breeding season the nest is lined with fishbones from the last or only brood, and with the protective quill sheaths of the feathers.

It was said that this 'cup' of fishbones was so delicate that it could not be handled without falling to pieces— and he who succeeded in carrying this marvel intact to the King of England would receive from that monarch a bag of gold. There was a tradition that the authorities of the British Museum were so anxious to secure a perfect example of this peculiar nest that they were willing to pay £100 for a specimen. No doubt such an offer inspired many a treasure-seeking enthusiast and indeed there are many accounts of how the kingfisher nest could be removed intact.

For our part, until 1963 we had only seen one nest. That year, when we started to film, we hoped that the pair might nest somewhere near our stream. But after a brief courtship display and a feeble attempt at excavating the all-too-stony bank, they both disappeared to nest somewhere else and did not reappear again at the stream, at least as regular visitors, till July.

Nevertheless we did have the opportunity of watching the procedure of events at one nest that was found by a local keeper in a rather unusual place—or so we thought then. It was in a chalk pit. Had this been a disused pit it would have seemed more normal, but there was a constant daily bustle for most of the week. The birds were nesting in an older part of the pit, but only a short distance away men were using excavators to remove the chalk from the banks, a lime-crushing plant was operating, and lorries were loading the finished lime only a few yards from the nest. Later the men told us that this or some other site in the pit had been used by the birds for many years. We climbed up a rubble-strewn bank to a platform under a place where there were two holes. The pit is all chalk (with lines of flints) except for a foot or a foot and a half of topsoil—in this case, hard red clay. It was in this clay, less than a foot from the surface, that the two holes were situated. One hole was very short with a flint blocking the way, and the other went in about eleven inches. At the end of this, we could see with the aid of a mirror some young kingfishers already in their spiky jackets who were at least a fortnight old.

Although we filmed them in the nest we were greatly disappointed that there were only four youngsters. It was quite possible that there had been more eggs, and that some had rolled out of the short tunnel during the incubation period, for the chamber lacked a good depression to keep them in. Altogether the parents' behaviour was out of keeping with that of a normal pair. The cock bird never brought fish to the nest, and indeed only appeared on one occasion—on the evening before the young were due to leave the nest, when he flew about the pit screaming. As there were only four birds to feed, and later two (for two ventured down the short tunnel too early, before they could fly, and fell to their deaths), this may have meant that only one parent needed to look after the brood. Or perhaps he was doing the fishing and handing over his catch to the hen who was only delivering. Unfortunately we were

A unique photograph of kingfishers mating

Youngster after leaving nest, not yet moulted. Notice its black feet and the tiny white spot at the tip of its beak

Female kingfisher. Its rose-coloured under-mandible is the only distinguishing external feature between the sexes

never able to prove or disprove this theory. So we filmed the four youngsters in the quill stage, but only two when fully feathered, which we thought would prove rather an anti-climax to the film. Worse, the colour stock we used was prone to colour cast, and the reddish-brown interior of the nest coloured the birds likewise. Disappointed, we waited at the pit hoping the kingfishers might have another brood, but they did not.

At the end of July, 1963, we went back to watching our kingfishers at the stream. At first there was only one—the old cock bird. During the first week of August we noticed that another one came there too. This one seemed very tame, for it would sit only a few yards from us and we could watch it fishing so long as we did not move. Its wings were a dull blue-green, and its feet were black. It was the latter feature that betrayed it. It was a juvenile, not yet moulted. At the tip of its beak there was a very tiny white spot. The bird would often sit on the handrail outside the water-keeper's cottage and the waterkeeper's wife once saw the young swallows bombarding it. Upstream in the cressbeds three more young kingfishers could be seen fishing together at times. During the following weeks 'our' young kingfisher lost its dull feathers and gained the new bright adult ones. The old cock bird rarely came down to fish; instead, another youngster also in the moult came down and fished amicably with the first one. This new bird had a light rose under-mandible—a female—and during the weeks that followed the black feet of both birds began to change: red blotches appeared, and finally they both had scarlet feet and black toenails.

This new female took great delight in driving the old cock bird away from the stream whenever she found him there, and would then take all the big fish for herself. Often she took fish that were too big and found she could not swallow them, eventually having reluctantly to drop them. Frequently the two young birds would fish together, and soon the old cock bird stopped appearing at all, so we assumed that the two youngsters had taken the territory.

During August we decided that if we were to get the two birds to nest the next year, we would have to do something about the bank. For three years the kingfishers had tried to excavate there, but the low and stony banks were hardly suitable. Finally we decided to build a decent bank of fine earth and no stones. It would have to have a sheer front and to achieve this meant placing something along the front of the bank while we were building it. We chose the west-facing bank of the stream and fixed a piece of box fence 10 feet long and 6 feet high in front of the bank.

Then we began the mammoth job of earth-moving. We had only shovels and buckets to work with and the earth had to be carried 50 yards to the bank. There was plenty of stony earth about the vicinity of the bank but this was not good enough. We dug back into the fine loam of the marshes until, shovel after shovelful and bucket after bucketful, by the end of the week-end we had reached 5 feet 6 inches, which was 3 feet higher than the existing bank. The mound went back 3 to 4 feet and we planted the top of it with a good layer of turfs. The fence was left in position for several weeks until the earth was settled. On removal we had a beautifully moulded bank, with a sheer face, free of stones, where a kingfisher could burrow out a good nest well above high-water level.

We were not sure that the birds would choose to nest there, but there was no other such fine bank in their whole fishing territory—at least, not one that was so free of water vole dwellings and flint.

It was worth the effort to try and attract them to it, and with luck they would hardly be able to turn a blind eye to it since they would (we hoped) fish there throughout the winter. We realised, however, that if they did nest there we could not expect them to continue the fishing, for kingfishers are said not to fish in the vicinity of the nest.

7

The First Brood

BY THE END of the year, 1963, we had everything ready, having done all we thought necessary to induce a pair of kingfishers to nest at our stream. The bank was built and had set well; at first we had feared that it might collapse, but although it had shrunk a little it seemed stable.

We kept the stream well stocked with fish, all through the winter. This was not much fun, especially catching bullheads. It was not so much the coldness of the water that made it unbearable, but rather our inability to hold the fish with such cold hands. Often it was easier to resort to catching the sticklebacks with the net. Still, the fish at the stream were easier to catch than those elsewhere and they still remained an effective attraction for the new pair of kingfishers.

It was on the 23rd December that we first saw the kingfishers, flying high above the tree-tops in their courtship flight. This amazed us, but the weather was very mild for the time of year. We saw their flights on two other occasions throughout January and not being sure how early they might begin to nest we kept a watchful eye upon the bank. We also inspected most of the banks in the cressbeds at intervals, but they were not so high as ours and most were riddled with water vole holes. It was almost unbearable even to think that the birds might nest in any other bank, and on reading an old account of how a photographer had started several holes for a pair of kingfishers where he wanted them to nest, and of his success, we followed his example in our bank.

Early February was still very mild. Behind the old mill, through last year's dead leaves, snowdrops sprang up, the single three-petalled flowers and the more beautiful double ones. Some of the birds had started to sing their spring songs, the hazel catkins along the hedge by the river dropped their long yellow tails, and the pussy willow began to bloom. The little yellow flowers of the celandine brightened up the dreariness of the riverside; and already the minnows were moving up into the shallow water.

When the kingfishers came down to the stream they usually arrived together. If one arrived before the other, it would often wait in the hedge by the hide, until the other came screaming downstream. They were particularly noisy when together like this, calling to each other 'Chee-ee, Chee-ee,' flying from perch to perch at the stream, first to the top grid then to the bottom, until they finally settled on perches facing each other or apart on the same perch. Any movement by one bird to get down to the other only resulted in the exchanging of positions again for another five minutes. Once settled the birds became intent upon the fish, watching for movements, and their excited whistles dropped back to a single chirp or 'pip.'

One morning the cock bird, who had taken his fill of four minnows, flew off. The hen, who had only taken one, became intent on a large bullhead. Such was this bird's passion for bullheads that she would try for one however large. This fish was about 3½ inches long, one we had found hiding beneath a rock under a small bridge where it had probably been for many years. When she had caught it she just gripped it by the tail, looking for all the world as though she would be sorry to drop it. But the young hen was cunning. The perch on which she sat was stout enough to knock the fish out on, but it overhung the water. She took a noticeably tighter grip upon the fish and carried it off to one of our bigger logs, the props that lay about upon the bank. This particular log did not overhang the water. Re-positioned, she began bashing, and once the struggle to kill the bullhead was over she found it an even bigger struggle to swallow. She did, somehow, but afterwards she rested a full five minutes, occasionally shaking her head and neck as if to settle the fish. Then she flew off towards the cressbeds in search of her mate.

With such an ideal opportunity to record the two birds calling we invested in a small battery-operated portable E.M.I. tape-recorder, a microphone and parabolic reflector.[1] With the 'dish' and the microphone set up upon the bank by the hide and directed at

---

[1] A parabolic reflector is a dish 3 feet across which amplifies all sound waves travelling into it, which are then bounced off its concave interior to the point of focus where the microphone picks them up.

the perch, we thought we might obtain some good recordings. We soon realised, however, that we would be picking up too much water noise from the grids and their hatches. For the slow-motion underwater filming sequence we had to increase the water noise by hanging tin cans in the waterfall current, for the high-speed camera had been noisy and we needed something consistently noisier nearer to the kingfisher perch to drown its motor noise.

Now we replaced the tin cans with old rags and mats to deaden the water noise. Unfortunately, the parabolic reflector picked up so many other miscellaneous noises that we had to dispense with it. Next day we set the open microphone under one of the kingfisher's perches. The cable stretched across the stream and led into the hide. This of course proved another good perching place for the birds. They flew excitedly about calling alternately and so fast that the overall noise was that of a burst of song. Unfortunately we were unable to monitor or play back the results until we got home to put the tape on a mains recorder, when we could hear the defects. The bird on the perch sitting over the microphone was too close and the other was too distant. Every time the bird on the perch dived into the water the microphone banged against it. The water noise was too loud, so the water would have to be stopped from flowing altogether by dropping the hatches which fed the stream.

Next morning I saw the waterkeeper and he dropped the hatches for us. Within half an hour there was only a little water trickling through. We attached the microphone to a fishing-rod which was suspended at an angle to deter the bird from using it as a perch, and by the middle of the afternoon we had recorded some better tapes.

It was on the first day we had begun to record that a rather surprising thing happened. Both birds were sitting on one perch, but the cock bird could not settle down. He flew to two other perches and then suddenly, quite without warning, he hurled himself at the bank. After dropping back he was quickly followed by the hen. The action was completely unexpected, but it was quite obvious that even at this early date, 24th February, nest building was in mind. We had, however, expected some kind of courtship display before they started excavating the actual hole. Even the previous owners of the stream had sat on the same perch together and bobbed and bowed to each other and fanned out their tails in alternate succession. Other reports say kingfishers have been known to hold or stroke bills, and the cock has been known to fly in small circles before the hen, dipping himself lightly upon the water. But with our two birds, there was no display but for this sudden burst of digging. This continued for some minutes. Each bird called excitedly and hurled itself at the bank, driving in its bill to loosen the soil. After this short attack upon the bank, they had made quite a noticeable depression, but the work had exhausted them. Both retired panting to the perch, and after a rest did a spot of fishing. The cock bird made four catches, but the hen missed all of hers and after ten minutes or so they began excavating again.

The cock was now hanging on to a root and pecking the bank in the manner that a woodpecker might use in making its hole, and the dirt was beginning to accumulate in the stream in a tell-tale heap. This pecking went on for several minutes at a time but then the cock dropped back to the perch and let the hen take over. After he had rested he dived several times on to the water to wash himself. He took some fish and then retreated to a comfrey stalk on the neighbouring side-stream where he spent five minutes preening, sometimes 'wash' diving on to the water. After this he disappeared in the direction of the cressbeds, but some time later came back for more excavating. By now it was fairly late afternoon and they dug in several places before going back to the original hole. When they had exhausted themselves, the cock was first to fly off, but the hen waited until she had caught a fish before she followed. Cramped but excited that they had accepted our bank, we crept out of the hide to examine the first hole. It was already two inches deep.

Now they had started digging they would probably go on till they had finished. But the next day the weather changed. The rain drizzled and an icy wind blew, and the birds did not dig much. By the middle of that week the hole only measured four inches deep. Then they had a spot of bad luck. The place they had chosen to dig was in the seam between the old and new banks. We had thought they would not go in as low as this, and they had the unfortunate luck to hit upon a large flint in the old bank. The flint was not a big one but they could not move it, so they began to build a new hole slightly higher up. They dug two or three inches a day and by Saturday (a week after starting the first hole) they were in eight inches. We had placed a mossy tree-stump in the stream in front of the holes as a convenient place for them to fly from. Once the excavating bird was out of sight in the hole, the other would sit outside on the log as if guarding. All the time it would call softly, reassuringly. The cock would stay in the hole for five minutes at a time, and the only evidence of his presence there was the occasional trickle of dirt which was rolling out of the hole and mounting in a heap under the hole. The kingfisher is a meticulously clean bird, and once it reappeared it proceeded to clean itself whilst the hen went into the hole to take her turn at digging. The tunnel was now beginning to rise upwards very slightly. By the time the birds had gone in ten inches they hit another stone. The cock bird came out frustrated and flustered, and in his anxiety flew into hole number one. Fortunately we had removed the stone blocking this one, and he came out calling excitedly. After flying in and out several times, he went on to excavate it. The hen, however, was rather put out by this reversion to the first hole, and would have nothing to do with it. Instead she went on to excavate a third hole of her own.

The next day, though, she must have reconsidered hole number one for when they came down to dig she sat outside on the log, guarding as before, calling softly, whilst he went on working, and she took her turn properly when he was exhausted. To excavate, the bird pecks the earth away with its beak, shovels it behind with its syndactyl feet, and then comes out of the hole backwards pushing the loose earth out with its tail. This last move may not necessarily be deliberate but the tail nonetheless becomes a convenient shovel.

When the cock bird had rested for a while he began to watch for the fish. He caught one and ate it, then caught another which he turned in his beak so that it was in the head-out position. It looked as if he might be going to feed the hen with it but she was out of sight digging in the hole and he readjusted the fish before swallowing it himself. When she did reappear he caught another and presented it to her headfirst, and after this first courtship feeding they flew up to the top of the pond, both diving in the water to bathe as they went. At the top of this pond, where the water flows in, there was always a shoal of minnows surging in the current. (Unfortunately they were too far away from the bank for us ever to catch any.) After watching them for a while the cock bird caught one and fed the hen again. This courtship feeding always involved the cock giving fish to the hen, never the reverse.

When they had finished they came back down to the bank for a while and the cock dug out a little more. That afternoon one bird kept appearing alone, then the other. Occasionally the waiting bird fished or sometimes preened first its chest, then its coverts, inside the wings and finally down the back. Most of the time, though, it spent waiting quietly.

About four o'clock they finally met again and resumed digging. It was a short burst because a group of people were walking across the field opposite on a public footpath, and their voices, although distant, disturbed the hen. She gave the alarm and the cock dropped out of the hole and both disappeared in an instant.

The next day the birds had more success and by the evening the tunnel measured 1 foot 6 inches. Now we finalised our plans. Once in the fine earth the birds would dig back another foot or so. They would not abandon the hole now for they were already far enough in to render their offspring safe from predators.

That evening about an hour before dark we set to work at the back of their bank. What we had to do would not interfere with the kingfishers since they did not dig in the evenings. It was essential for our filming purposes to organise the bank in such a way that we would not have to dig down to the finished nest to bring the young birds in range of the camera, which would have been a clumsy operation. About 2 feet 6 inches from the back of the bank we arranged a wooden framework, part of which included a wooden door with latches on, to go directly in line with the tunnel. This framework was placed at a slight angle to the tunnel so as to give the best angle for filming in the—as yet unmade—nest. When the kingfishers had dug another foot they would come across the board. Unable to go in any farther, and not needing to anyway, they would probably form the nest chamber right in front of the door. We wedged the board in with earth and stones, covering the top of the bank with plastic sheeting to keep the rain out, and then waited.

For a further week the kingfishers were busy in the tunnel. One day the cock bird came out of the hole head-first instead of with his usual backwards drop, and we knew then that he had formed the nesting chamber, for there was now enough room for him to turn around. That evening when all was quiet, we examined the back of the hole. On removing the door we found that the birds had indeed finished the chamber, which was right in front of the board. All we had to do when the time came was to replace the door with a window through which we could film the nestlings. We put everything back into place until the time came for filming.

Good Friday that year dawned cold. The cock bird was spending a lot of time in the hole, and when together the birds seemed little interested in the fish, only in their nest. They kept flying in and out. Then they would wash and preen. We were not sure if there were any eggs by then but, looking back on the hatching dates, there must have been although the birds were not staying in the hole long enough to incubate. But like many other species, as we discovered later, kingfishers do not incubate until the clutch is complete.

Next morning the cock bird came flying downstream and landed in the hedge by the hide. From there he called to the hen, who was in the nest. After a few seconds she came down to the edge of the tunnel and peered out cautiously. Reassured she flew out on to the perch, whereupon the cock left the hedge and came towards her. In his beak he held a minnow. The cock presented the fish to his mate and when he had fed her she sat in a curious upright position with her wings drooped and juddering. She was making a staccato bleating call, inviting him to mate with her. Ron was rewinding the camera furiously so as not to miss it. The cock hovered over her momentarily, then landed on her back, holding on to her nape feathers with his bill and at the same time flapping hard to keep balance. The hen moved her tail around sideways and coition took place. After this he flew away to the cress-beds, but she stayed on the perch for a full fifteen

minutes, when he returned with a fish for her. Then
she returned to the nest.

That same afternoon he called her out of the nest
again and fed her a large bullhead. Not once did he go
into the nest himself that day: altogether he fed her four
times. The birds never caught and ate fish outside the
nest; now they took the fish away into a nearby tree
to eat them. It seemed as though the birds did not
wish to draw any attention to the whereabouts of the
nest.

During this first week of egg-laying the hen often
came out of the nest quietly, fished, and took her catch
into the tree to eat. Her usual meal was two fish, after
which she returned to the nest for another hour. Once
she speared a fish. This is a most unusual thing for a
kingfisher to do, and it happened by accident. She
could do nothing with a fish caught like this and she
took it away to the tree to dislodge it. Once this was
done she returned, took two more fish, and went back
into the nest. Next time she came out she had fish
bones on her beak, which meant she must have been
turning or moving the eggs. The eggs are not
originally laid on fishbones but upon the bare soil, but
after the hen has regurgitated a lot of pellets the fishbones soon intermingle with the eggs, and if an observer were to look into the nest at this stage he would
naturally assume that the eggs had been laid on a bed
of fishbones.

When the cock bird returned the hen was still sitting
upon the perch, so he went inside. What his actions
there were is hard to imagine. It must have been too
dark for him to see anything; to feel if there were any
eggs he would have to climb over them. He had

obviously no intention yet of helping with the incubation and he soon reappeared. His presence immediately stirred the hen and she sat bolt upright, pulling the feathers close to her body. But they only called to each other before he flew away. We had not seen them mate since Easter Sunday, now in all probability we wouldn't again for we could only spend week-ends and evenings, with the occasional half-day holiday, at the stream. It is normally assumed that the birds mate once to fertilise eggs, not once a day to produce one egg at a time. Subsequent, if any, matings are probably purely for pleasure.

The hen was now spending as long as 75 minutes in the hole before reappearing. When she did come out she displayed even more caution and went to sit in the hedge. Within ten minutes the cock came from the direction of the cressbeds and went into the nest without reappearing. The hen then flew off to the cressbeds: he was now sharing the incubation with her.

Next day the hen showed even more caution before entering the nest, and after the cock had flown away she sat in the hedge and looked about her. After some time she came down to the perch by the nest, listened, and then disappeared in a flash.

The birds were changing over regularly now. On average the hen spent about 30 minutes more in the nest than the cock. She had $1\frac{3}{4}$ hours to his $1\frac{1}{4}$. It seemed that this was not because the cock bird shirked his duty, but rather because the hen was always anxious to get back, or perhaps knew some better and quicker fishing than he did. Now the changeover was regular, a definite pattern was adopted for it. The approaching mate would call in flight as it came downstream and the sitting mate would appear instantly, call a greeting to the other, and fly off quickly in the direction of the cressbeds.

The first week of incubation was nearly over, and with two more to go we spent little time there so as not to disturb them, and concentrated our filming upon other things: spring locations, the swans on their nest, the grey wagtail, and the fish.

It was not until the 16th April that things began to happen again. About 1.30 that Saturday afternoon we saw the birds flying around together. One of them seemed to be carrying a fish. After only fourteen days away from the stream it seemed to us that the plants on the path were twice the height as before, for they hindered us in our anxious rush to get to the hide as fast as possible. We dived breathlessly into the hide and waited. Within ten minutes one bird came back and went into the hole. Another ten minutes elapsed and then it reappeared with an eggshell in its beak. The eggs had hatched. We trained the camera on the hole, hoping to film one of the birds bringing out an egg-shell. But this was so unpredictable an event that when it happened we missed it, for the bird was already at the edge of the tunnel and ready to fly out by the time our reflex action had caught up with it. The bird did not deposit the eggshell outside the nest but flew upstream and dropped it in the pond before disappearing to the cressbeds. Here myriads of tiny sticklebacks had hatched. They were not hard to find and the king-fisher lost no time in choosing one. Meanwhile his mate had already returned to the nest with a very tiny fish, head presented outwards, ready for the nestlings' first feed. The bird must have caught it in such a hurry that it had not even stopped to kill it. It now paused to do so before entering the nest. The young open their beaks automatically when a parent approaches with food. Before many seconds had passed the hen reappeared and stopped for a bathe and preen. Soon the cock bird returned with another fish. As the pattern unfolded, it seemed as though one bird would feed, then remain with the brood until the other returned. And so on.

Next afternoon, when both parents were absent from the nest for a few minutes, we decided to peep in at the babies. The weather was mild or we would not have risked looking so early. Behind the door were five pink nestlings, so small and arranged in such a tangle that it was difficult to know which head belonged to which body. They had long necks and were very ugly: their eyes were closed and bulged out from beneath their skin. They were completely featherless and must have grown considerably since the previous afternoon, for it was hard to see how even this small nestling could have come out of so small an egg. Amongst them was one other egg, as yet unhatched. They huddled together for warmth and support, for they lacked the strength to keep their heads up for very long. They measured about $1\frac{1}{2}$ inches long.

We covered them in again and returned to the hide. Very soon the hen bird returned and went in, where she remained to brood and to await her mate's arrival. When the fishing parent came downstream he called and the hen left the nest, clearing the way for him to go straight in and remain there to brood until she came back. Two days later we took out the unhatched egg from amongst the nestlings. It was addled and chipped. Underneath them we found yet another egg, the seventh. It was still as clear, pink, and translucent as the day it had been laid, but it was infertile. Then we closed the nest. We had decided to film the birds for the first time when they were a fortnight old and in the quill stage. We could film nestlings at an earlier stage on the second brood (if any). However, there was a surprise in store for us, and they were never to reach that age.

The adult birds fed the young well up to the eleventh day. On the twelfth we visited the hide as we did every evening. Normally, by putting one's ear to the entrance hole of the nest, one could hear the youngsters calling. Now it was deadly quiet. We decided to look into the nest to see if they were all right. We expected to find them asleep. Instead we could scarcely believe our eyes. Some terrible disaster had befallen them. Their collapsed bodies lay in a heap in the nest: they were dead—for how long was hard to say. Perhaps several hours. We removed them and examined each body carefully. There were no marks upon three of them. On the fourth was a tiny spot of blood. The fifth was missing. At this stage the birds still had no feathers, although the sheaths with the feathers inside were clearly visible beneath the skin and would have soon broken through. The fifth youngster lay in the stream beneath the nest. He could not have wandered out of the nest for his eyes were not yet open. It must have been pulled out of the nest. Its skin was bleeding and torn in several places.

Our first concern lay with the parents. Perhaps one had been shot, or caught by a predator. As their feeding grounds were the cressbeds we went straight there and were relieved to hear them both calling somewhere in the distance. We thought we might find out more relating to the tragedy if we watched from the hide.

We had not been sitting there long before the hen bird came down. She looked very dejected, but she caught a fish and then after a while flew off. Some time later the cock bird arrived. Twice he flew into the nest and then he flew at the bank. Surely he was not building another nest? When he had flown back to the cressbeds we examined the place that he had flown at and found under the overhang a new hole, already four inches deep. They had wasted no time over the tragedy. It had not broken their relationship or curbed their urge to breed.

The fact that we had found one of the youngsters in the stream would suggest that they had tried to clear the old hole out, and being unsuccessful had started a new one. One would not have thought it such a difficult job to drag the youngsters out, unless for some reason they now feared this nest. Perhaps some rat or predator had got inside. Whatever the cause there was no evidence to suggest a clear-cut explanation, and as it was getting near dusk we removed the four bodies from the nest and buried them behind the bush: a rather unexpected end to the kingfisher's first brood.

The next lunchtime, still low-spirited about this recent development, we went over to the stream. Somewhere in the vicinity came a rather unusual noise. Fairly similar to the robin's aggressive 'tick' it was definitely an anger note, a continuous guttural ticking or almost grunting sound. But there was no bird to be seen and we did not then associate it with king-fishers.

But that evening was an enlightening one. The kingfishers were still calling to each other in the cress-beds as we made our way over to the hide. It would not be long before they came to the stream, as they always did just before dusk.

We had been watching only a few minutes when the birds came flying across the stream and circled around. There was definitely something amiss—now there were three kingfishers, not two! Even at the speed they were flying it was possible to distinguish three shapes.

After a while the cock bird came down to the perch. He was making a terrible noise. It was, in fact, the same noise that we had heard at lunchtime: 'Shrit-it-it!' We heard another bird answer in the same tones. These were not the kingfisher's usual harmonious ones. Soon the truth dawned. One was an intruder. This other kingfisher, also a cock bird, sat a little farther down-stream. Their positions were not at all relaxed. Their notes were territorial, angry. Suddenly both birds left their perches and began swooping at each other viciously. Off they went chasing each other.

Each bird chose a perch eight to ten yards apart. Facing each other they sat upright with wings drooping and head moving about in a slow exaggerated fashion; the bill pointed viciously and moved meaningfully from side to side. Then they lay flat along the perch. When one thought the other was off guard he would fly at him in an attempt to knock him off the perch, attempting to grasp hold of his opponent's bill in the fray and drag him into the water. If he succeeded the unfortunate bird would experience a ducking. We watched as much of the fight as we could from the hide, though we had rather a restricted view. The hen kept well out of it but was somewhere nearby. This was perhaps the finale, for next morning the intruder was nowhere to be seen and the birds acted normally again.

The intruder must have been making his way back up the river after wintering on the estuary, and was now looking for a mate and a territory, both of which would be fought for if necessary. It should be remembered that our pair of kingfishers had begun to nest exceptionally early, when, indeed, other kingfishers had not even begun courtship display or nesting. This intruder had disturbed them and, being first-year birds, they were not yet experienced enough to deal with such a situation. Therefore, instead of the hen continuing to feed the young, she left them. Or perhaps they had both been involved in an earlier fight. In either case the young had been left too long to be saved from exhaustion. Once exhausted through hunger they will not ask for food, and one parent, thinking the other had satisfied their offspring's needs, would not bother to feed them. Had they tried to present any food to the young in their weak state the fish would have been dropped in the nest alongside them. But none were found, so it is probably correct to assume that the parents had not even attempted to feed the young that day.

Unfortunately, as the fight had taken place in the evening, we were not able to film this behaviour. Had we realised what the 'odd noise' was that lunchtime we could have spent the rest of the day waiting in the hide.

The whole of April had been given to the three weeks of hatching and eleven days of feeding the young, the date now, the day after the fight, being 1st May. The kingfishers seemed determined to go and breed and still had plenty of time. The breeding season can be an extended one, for it is not unusual to find them still breeding in September.

Although the original nest was empty and the birds kept flying in and out of it they still did not seem enthusiastic about it. Most of the early morning they spent sitting on opposite perches looking at each other. There were no signs yet of the intruder, and although the birds called to each other from time to time it was not with their usual enthusiasm.

They seemed unable to decide whether to go on cleaning out the old nest or to excavate a new one. The hen seemed interested in the new one as she kept flying in to excavate it, but the cock seemed to want to go ahead and clear out the old one now that it was empty. Later that morning he stayed inside for long spells, eventually emerging with dirt on his beak. He bathed on leaving the hole by belly-flopping several times upon the water, then preening and shuffling his wings to complete his toilet.

All day long little time was spent elsewhere. Only occasionally did the kingfishers go to the cressbeds. The hen at one stage tried to induce the cock bird to mate, and chased him around playfully.

The next day it seemed that the decision had been taken. The cock bird spent a long time in the old nest cleaning it out. By late afternoon all the fishbones that had been in the chamber were scattered on the face of the bank, and he was so busy making a thorough job of it that he did not even stop to wash or preen.

On examination late that evening we found that there

was not one fishbone left in the chamber. The earth was bare, with a deepish depression, once more. If it were true that the kingfisher deliberately lays its eggs on a bed of fishbones surely they would have gone straight ahead with the egg-laying instead of carrying out these elaborate cleaning measures.

8

Second and Third Broods

ALL NEXT DAY the hen waited patiently, uttering her
'chee-chee' softly. When the cock had eventually
finished clearing out the nest he flew off, not even
stopping for a bathe or preen, no doubt heading for
the cressbeds for a meal after so much work.

She waited for a while, then dashed into the hole.
What she did once inside one can only imagine;
possibly she shuffled around in the nest depression and
settled down to test its comfort. When she came back
down the tunnel she did not dash out directly as usual,
but instead came down to the entrance and peered out
cautiously. Whether she feared to betray her nesting-
place or whether this was merely a case of the satisfied
female examining the view, it is hard to say.

Satisfied then, she dropped out and disappeared
through the trees. Soon afterwards the cock returned.
He had brought a fish to feed her, but obviously she
had not expected one so soon or else she would have
waited. Although he sat for a long time patiently
waiting she did not reappear, and he flew off with it.
No doubt he found her. Later that evening both birds

came down the river together. They had come to fish at the pool. Within a few minutes, without a courtship feeding and without any invitation from her at all, they mated.

By 6th May, there were two eggs in the nest and by the 9th, five. When we examined them, the first we had seen, we found them to be a delicate pink, but once incubation began their appearance changed to a chalky white. They were almost round and measured just under three-quarters of an inch. For the first few days during egg-laying, the hen did not spend much time in the nest. On the 10th May the cock was still calling her out of the nest and feeding her, and mating usually resulted. By this time we had been lucky enough to film the courtship feeding three times and the mating twice.

We watched at fairly regular intervals during the three weeks of incubation, and saw that the birds changed over as before during the day. We were interested to find out which one of them sat on the eggs all night, and it proved to be the hen.

On the 29th May, we set up our equipment again at the pool for we knew that the kingfishers' second clutch of eggs were near hatching. We had not spent any time at all filming the kingfishers during the last nineteen days, for during incubation there is little action, only at changeover times when the birds appear at the nest site for a few brief moments.

On our way to the kingfisher 'set' we had to pass the pond and we paused, as we always did, to look for shoals of minnows. As we peered into the water we saw something white lodged among the fronds of ranunculus. It was a broken eggshell and farther down there were more of these. There was not a perceptible current to carry the shells away and they remained probably not far from where the kingfishers had dropped them. We collected the eggshells for future filming, and then went to watch from the hide.

The parent kingfishers were once again taking very tiny fish into the nest and all seemed well. We decided there and then to film the young kingfishers at a week old. It would be too risky from our previous observation of their development to film them before this time, but by the seventh day they would be sturdy enough to be filmed. There were five young in the nest and one infertile egg.

The nest was already accessible for filming but we had to fix an extension on the front of our hide and take it across the stream and behind the nest bank. We laid two iron rails across the stream and rolled the hide across and placed the front of it five feet away from the door at the back of the nest. We could not film looking straight into the back of the nest from the hide without there being some kind of lightproof tunnel between the two. We spent several hours building the wooden tunnel behind the trees so that we would not disturb the birds feeding. One end of the tunnel was larger than the other. The nest end was tapered down to the size of the door at the back of the nest. The end that abutted on to the hide was about $2\frac{1}{2}$ to 3 feet square.

The tunnel was painted black inside. When the birds were absent from the nest site we erected the extension from the back of the nest and fixed it to the front of the hide. Inside the tunnel about halfway along were two lamps—375-watt reflector photofloods.

We had already laid on an electricity supply. Seventy-five yards away was the waterkeeper's cottage, and from there we laid a cable across the field. It was tied for the most part to the trees that line the river-bank, and then to the hide. The supply fed into a transformer and then out to the two lamps in the tunnel. The transformer was a variable one so that we could fade in our lights gradually to accustom the birds to them. We dared not use more than two lamps because of the heat they generate. Even these two provided only minimum lighting conditions of f3-5—on High Speed Ektachrome E.R., which is rated at 125 A.S.A.

The camera was set up by mid-day and we were ready to film. The door of the nest was removed and a perspex window replaced it. As yet all was still in darkness. We let the parent feed again before starting to fade in the lights.

At seven days the young birds were only being brooded occasionally, once every 1½ to 2 hours. They had no feathers yet but these were clearly visible under the skin in various places—on the wings, down the centre of their backs, and on their chests. They were still blind but could stand now on their own two feet holding their heads up—an untidy bunch, ugly and awkward. By filming them through a window we were cutting out any unnecessary draughts. Once the lights were on the birds might gain a little heat from them to keep them warm.

A sudden shriek came from outside: a parent was returning. Breathlessly we faded in the lights to an almost imperceptible dimness, and the parent came in and went out followed by its mate.

Next time, now acclimatised to that small amount of light, we faded them up a little more. After two hours of this procedure, increasing the light after both parents had visited, we had the lights fully on. In fact we found towards the end that it was all right to increase the brightness of the lights whilst the parents were still in the nest, for it caused no concern. At two hundred and forty volts and 3,200° Kelvin—the lights at full power —we began filming. Fortunately from that distance, behind a window and the wall of the hide, there was no camera noise to worry the birds.

We did not have the lights on full when the parent kingfishers were absent but kept them very dim, mainly for the youngsters' sake; if we had not done so we would have had to be constantly cleaning the perspex window, for it is the habit of young kingfishers to excrete in the direction of the light source, down the nest hole. Since our lights now constituted the strongest light source they excreted in that direction. After this had happened two or three times we caught on and kept the camera lights so dim that the birds went back to their normal toilet habits. They sat facing the light coming up the natural tunnel, and once the camera lights came on full they sat facing these.

When one nestling was hungry it would start calling. Soon it awakened the rest and they all called, making a non-stop din. The parents came in with a fish already held head outwards and would present this towards them; the nearest one would open its beak as soon as the fish touched it.

At seven days old, the birds were taking much bigger fish than we had anticipated. Some indeed were almost as long as the chick and we became quite concerned for one youngster. The fish it had been fed was a bullhead and was so big that we thought it could not possibly swallow it. But it did, or at least it swallowed almost all of it, the rest protruding for over a quarter of an hour, during which time the bird sat completely upright with the tail still in its beak. After a while the fish began to digest and we could see from where we were the form of the fish going into the gullet. Once fed and satisfied, the nestling moved to the back of the bunch and went to sleep.

Once, the cock came back and after feeding stayed to brood. This was a charming sight. Somehow he shuffled his way through or over the young birds until most of them were under him, and then he fluffed out his feathers and drooped his wings over them and remained like this for ten minutes or so. The young were by no means still whilst being brooded; suddenly a head might appear, or some feet, and then there would be a general shuffle around until once again they would settle down.

We took various shots that day, some of the cock bird bringing in fish and feeding, and some of the hen. In one shot she dropped her fish and groped about unsuccessfully on the floor for it. And there were other shots of the hen brooding. We filmed mid-shots and close-ups, and concluded the sequence with big close-ups of the youngsters. As there was little other action we decided they had been exposed to the light long enough, so we turned off the lights to let the parents feed in the dark again. They did this with no trouble, so we put the door back in and covered everything over to wait a further week, when the youngsters would have grown and acquired their spiky jackets.

We kept an eye on the birds every evening and after fourteen days there was a considerable difference in their size and appearance. Also their eyes were open. We think that this happened about the twelfth day. Their feathers had burst through but were enclosed in quills; these would split and their feathers would emerge before twenty-one days were through. The quills gave them an armoured appearance, like medieval soldiers in chain mail. They were very amiable with each other, never pecking or quarrelling. They lined up with military precision, hungriest birds to the fore of the chamber, calling madly, and once having received their rations moved to the back of the queue. The parents did not need to come right into the chamber now; they came only to the entrance where the presented fish was eagerly taken. Before this the parents had always come into the chamber, found the birds and fed them, and then turned around, leaving the nest head-first. Now they merely backed down the tunnel, dropped out at the end, half-turning as they dropped, and flew rapidly off to bathe, for by now the narrow tunnel was very well whitewashed, filthy and slippery, and the parents soiled their feathers as they passed through. One thing we did notice was that the parent on entering the tunnel grunted or croaked, presumably to attract the nestlings' attention.

On the fourteenth day we were set up and ready to film very early in the morning—7.30 a.m. The time passed. We thought that the birds would be fed between 9 and 9.30 a.m., but the parents did not return until 11.30, when they both came bringing a fish each to feed two of the nestlings. The lights were not upsetting them but something had disrupted their normal routine.

Before mid-day we had realised the cause of the trouble. The owners of the cressbeds had this very day decided to start excavating to extend their beds. For this they were using an excavator and subsequently an enormous amount of mud was flung out of the cressbeds via the kingfishers' fishing haunts, and it was impossible to see any fish in the waters at all. There were plenty of fish in the stream outside the nest but some instinct stopped the birds fishing there.

As it seemed very unlikely that the other three babies were going to be fed for some time we fed them ourselves before we went to lunch. It is unlikely they were fed in our absence of about half an hour, and it was as well that we did feed them for the parents did not reappear until 4.30 p.m. and then only made three visits. Perhaps the men had stopped the excavation and were having a tea-break. At about 5 o'clock the excavator started working again and finally at 8 p.m., it stopped work for the day. Now the water began slowly to clear and the parents brought a further two fish before dusk. Assuming that the nestlings had all been fed before 7.30 a.m. they would barely have had two to three fish each that day had we not fed them as well. Afraid that what they had eaten that day was not enough to keep them from weakening we gave them each as many as they could take—two or three big fish each, which would keep them through the night.

Next day the excavator was not working and the

parents were in and out of the nest every twenty minutes, in strong contrast to the day before.

By now the tunnel was very slippery and filthy. Each time a parent came out it went to bathe. These cleaning dives took two forms. If the parents still had several more youngsters to feed, they merely took two or three quick dips into the water on their way across the pond towards the fishing grounds. If they had finished feeding for a while, all the nestlings being fast asleep on heavy stomachs, the bathing was a lengthy business: several bellyflops on to the water to wet themselves, then a full preen of all their breast- and wing-feathers. Then they flew off to catch a fish for themselves. With these charming actions occurring every half hour on perches up and down the pond we were able to film good bathing sequences, complete with preening, and from every angle. We simply moved the hide up and down the banks whilst the birds were absent.

We decided that a few shots of the birds killing bullheads and turning them would be useful and easy to film now they were fishing so regularly—if they could be induced to fish near the nest.

We put some big bullheads in a bowl and placed them in a shallow zinc bath above the stream at one corner of the pond, the corner they most frequently used for bathing. The cock bird immediately started to take from the supply. He fished from the new stout log we had set up, a good table for bashing bullheads upon. It was not long before the hen returned and found him fishing there. They called excitedly to each other all the while, for up to now they had been so busy fishing in different parts of their territory that they

Kingfisher with bullhead: the female clasps the fish just above the tail, before presenting it head-first to one of her young

KINGFISHER NESTLINGS
at seven days old:
eyes closed, completely
featherless, they huddle
together for warmth and
support

At fourteen days old:
the quill stage

The parent bird at the
nest entrance feeds the
young, who call out
hungrily

scarcely saw much of each other. Indeed the appearance
of her mate excited the hen to such an extent that when
he brought a fish to the perch outside the nest, prior to
entering, she sidled up to him expecting to be fed.
When she found he was not going to give her the
fish she tried to take it from him, but he, quick as a
flash, disappeared into the nest. When he came back
out she chased him, and after courtship feeding they
copulated.

By 4.30 p.m. the birds had taken all the fish out of
the zinc bath and when the last one had gone, they disappeared in the direction of the cressbeds to resume
fishing there. Usually they fished from the short
walls separating the beds, watching for a large stickleback among the myriads of small ones. Fishing now
was very easy, there was no shortage, and, with the
young kingfishers due out of the nest soon, fish that
were easy to catch were a necessity.

That evening we caught some more bullheads and
put them in the zinc bath. When the cock bird returned it was 7.30 p.m. and the sight of the bullheads
made him very excited. He peered over the perch at
them, first turning his head one way, then running
down the perch to the farthest point and craning his
head over to watch them—almost to the point of over-
balancing. He sidled up and down the perch and it
seemed almost as if he could not make up his mind
which to take first. Eventually he dived upon one,
caught it and took it to the nest. When the hen
arrived they both fished fast, furiously, and successfully,
taking nine fish into the nest in well under ten minutes,
and then took two or three each for themselves. Having emptied the bowl the work was done for the day.

By putting fish there for them to take we ensured that they fed their young in the evenings at least. We could not let the youngsters starve if the excavator was stopping the parents from finding fish, also we had one more nest sequence yet to film—that of the young birds fully feathered.

The next day the excavator had started working again. But we were prepared. The fish the birds had taken from the bowl the evening before were not all that we had caught that day. We still had about thirty left. We made a container of perforated zinc which was anchored in the stream behind the grid, and this contained the rest of the catch. We had had to think ahead, for we could not have found and caught any bullheads in muddy water any more than the kingfishers could have done. This supply lasted them most of the day, at least while the excavator was working. We had to replenish the supply in the evening and as usual we watched the action from the hide. It was not long before the cock bird appeared. He took eight fish into the nest and fed himself, all within the space of five minutes: a record perhaps!

With more fish supplied the cock fed the youngsters next day, and in the evening it was the hen bird who found the next new supply. She fed the whole brood, and then herself. It is always interesting how the parent birds will always make sure that the brood is fully fed before they eat themselves.

The hen, having finished fishing, turned her attention to the bank. She flew at it—just once—driving in her bill. Was she starting another nest?

During the two evenings that followed, we constantly saw the birds flying at the bank, but never more than two or three times at once, so we thought that it was not serious excavation. But on examination later we found that there was a new tunnel already 1 foot 4 inches long. They must have been very busy these past days feeding the young and themselves, and building a new nest. It seemed rather amazing that they were actually concerned with digging a new nest before their first successful brood had flown. For the young, now fully feathered, still had four or five days to remain in the nest.

When the youngsters were twenty-one days old we decided to film them again. It was as well we chose that day for filming, for it was the last day that the hen took any interest in feeding them. She rarely fed them at all after twenty-two days; instead she concentrated on digging the new nest.

The fully-feathered young were now looking more like their parents. They were duller, especially around the wings and breast. The blues of the head and wings and tail were a dull cobalt, and the breast was a pale rusty brown, instead of the glowing, fiery orange of the adult. The whites were dirty and slightly tinged with rusty brown. Their beaks were black and still fairly short, having about another half-inch to grow. The feet were black, too, and they remained so until after their autumn moult. The only colour that was accurately matched with the parents was the azure streak of their backs, and likewise the two rows of azure speckles on each wing and across the head. The nest seemed full up now. A lot of time was spent in preening and stretching first one wing, then the other. The young birds did not quarrel or peck each other as some young birds are inclined to do, nor did they wander off down

99

the tunnel; instead, they kept to the precincts of the chamber.

After the hen bird had ceased feeding the young on the Saturday, the cock bird was working twice as hard. We felt rather sorry for him and on the Sunday we gave him a hand by making the fishing easier for him. There was little filming that could be done at this stage and so we spent a good deal of time catching fish and putting them in the zinc bath under the bathing perch.

The following day was the 25th day after hatching and we expected to find an empty nest by the end of the day, but only two had left, one at 12 noon, and the other at 4 p.m. We wanted to record the departure for the film but it proved a fairly impossible task. If the parent had called them out of the nest, as we had previously thought might happen, or if there had been any preliminary warning of a bird emerging, we would have stood a chance. So the whole day was spent waiting in the hope that by some freak of luck we might be able to tell when one was on the point of leaving. Meanwhile we could watch the hen bird, who was busy digging.

She was resting on the perch after a hard spell excavating when the second youngster emerged. He fluttered only a few feet over the water and then fell into it, and she just sat there watching. She must have seen the youngster struggling, and we thought she was going to help it: but no, she flew off. We emerged from the hide to help the poor creature who was now quite wet. Fortunately there was not a strong current so had we not been there it would probably have been able to struggle to the edge of the stream and rest on the bank. We put it on the perch to dry off. About three-quarters of an hour later it had made no move so we decided it would have a better chance of survival if it spent the night in the nest.

By late afternoon the next day the remaining youngsters were scattered up and down the riverside. We knew they were there although at first they were hard to spot. They were keeping fairly high in the trees of the opposite bank, and their drab colours mixed very well with their surroundings. They chiefly betrayed their whereabouts with bobbing movements and a single chirp uttered from time to time. Had we been able to get nearer to them we would have been able to see them blinking too. The one we had handled the previous afternoon had blinked hard at intervals, its eyes having to accustom themselves to the constant bright light (though when we had filmed them with the lights on I cannot remember having seen them blink). We wondered what dangers would befall these youngsters now they were having to fend for themselves in the big wide world. They seemed to have very little idea of the whereabouts of the fish, for they sat looking heavenwards. The normal kingfisher stance is always to look down into the water. And they would have to be very careful if they were going to fish the river, for the currents run very strongly in some parts. No doubt a lucky escape from such a current would be their first lesson and they would soon find less dangerous and more shallow waters to fish.

Although we never saw either of the parents attempting to feed the young as we thought they might, at least two of the brood survived and occasionally turned up near the old nest area during the summer.

It was now fairly certain that the kingfishers were going to produce yet another brood. We used the same back-of-the-nest procedure as we had used with the first nests, so as to observe what was going on inside, and the following day, 24th June, an egg was deposited upon the floor of the new nesting chamber. We took this opportunity of filming the egg in the nest. Then we filmed again when there were three and five eggs.

The very fact that the kingfishers were nesting again was fascinating and quite a rare occurrence. On glancing through literature on the subject there seem to be only two similar cases. The first was in Renfrewshire in 1934; the first brood (7) were nearly ready to fly when the second clutch (7) was completed in a second nest hole. But by the time the second brood had reached the fledgling stage a third clutch of seven eggs had already been incubated for a week in the first nest. This is a fine record.

A pair of Swedish birds had a similar experience. The young of the first brood were nine days old when the first egg of the second clutch was laid. The observer felt there was something odd because the cock bird had a habit of disappearing for a few hours after feeding the first brood. It was eventually discovered that he was in fact incubating a second brood and then dashing back to feed the first. Then when the second brood of young had reached twelve days old he was left to finish rearing them on his own.

Eventually after laying an egg a day there were six eggs in our birds' new nest, and the hen began to incubate. The cock fed her outside the nest during the first few days, and she would sometimes fly about the area for a few minutes. Within a few days they were back to the old routine of sharing the incubation and changed over regularly every two to three hours.

Old records tell us that the urge for a nest site may drive kingfishers who have no nesting territory to nest very close to other pairs. On one occasion on a Scottish river there were two pairs already nesting very close together, with an old empty hole between them. Both pairs had overhauled the hole before deciding upon a new one of their own. This middle hole was eventually taken over by a third pair of kingfishers who successfully completed a clutch of seven eggs. By this time the nests on either side contained well-developed young. One day when the owners of the middle hole were absent from the area their eggs, which were still fresh, were cleared out of the nest by the other king-fishers.

At another site six young were being successfully reared when another pair took possession of a bank one hundred and fifty yards away. They excavated, laid their eggs, and had completed two weeks of incubation when the first pair returned, after two weeks' absence from the area, obviously bent upon rearing another brood. They inspected both holes and cleared them out. Unfortunately the eggs of their neighbours were near hatching, but after clearing out their neighbours' eggs they returned to their own nest and deposited their second clutch. It is unlikely that they resented the other pair's intrusion, otherwise they would have evicted them earlier. The more likely explanation is that as they cleared the nest out in the dark, so they mistook the eggs for mere objects or things to be re-moved out of the way.

Since our off-duty kingfisher had nothing to do but catch fish for himself we devised one or two 'sets' and backgrounds. 'Private Fishing' notices abound up and down the Test and since they make an ideal perching place from which to fish we decided that our master fisherman must be portrayed on one. So we set one up where the kingfisher used to bathe. Underneath was the usual complement, the bath of bullheads. This made for a very amusing sequence. An even funnier shot would have been of something the waterkeeper saw. The kingfisher was sitting on the perch with his head sideways and a quizzical expression in his eye, looking towards the 'Private Fishing' notice on which a grey wagtail was resting. It is a funny thing but the kingfisher never likes to see any other bird on its favourite perch and will often push the intruder off. In this case it did look rather as if the kingfisher was thinking, 'can't you read?'

The third clutch hatched on the 18th July, the first notice we had being the broken eggshell that had been dropped in the pond. On examining the nest when both parents were absent we found complete success—six out of six. We wanted to film the eggs hatching but this was something we dared not do. The young when first hatched are so very weak that the slightest draught might kill them or the slightest disturbance may cause the parents to desert. It is a risk that no bird-loving photographer dare take, not even in the cause of science or scientific record.

Our kingfishers' lives were full of disastrous and dangerous events without us causing more. The first had been the intruder, the second the muddy water which prevented them from fishing when they most

needed to. The third occurred when the new brood
was seven days old. It was a Sunday. We spent all
day in the vicinity of the kingfisher stream and during
the whole of the day the hen was absent. At first we
did not take much notice. We could easily have
missed her. By the evening we realised that the cock
bird had only taken two fish into the nest. We were
worried then. About 7.30 we decided that it was unlikely now that the young were going to get another
fish between them, and once again we decided to feed
them to help them survive the night. We gave them as
much as they could eat and closed them in for the night.

On his way back over the stream's small bridge, a
railway sleeper near the top grid, Ron happened to look
down at the grid. The concrete pillars that hold the iron
are slotted twice with a small space between them. The
first slot holds the grid and the first baffleboards, which
control the water level in the pond. The second slot
holds the second baffleboards, which let the water
drain slowly into the stream.

There in the narrow space between the two was our
missing kingfisher. Wet and bedraggled she sat
miserably hunched up, unable to open her wings in the
narrow space to fly out. What baffled us was how she
managed to get herself into such a position in the first
place. The poor bird must have been there all day.
Probably she had caught a fish near there and had taken
it to the board to kill it, then accidentally dropped it
behind the board. Seeing it there she had thought-
lessly jumped down to pick it up. Having secured it
she found herself in a very odd situation, unable to
open her wings wide enough to get out. Perhaps she
struggled. If she did it was surprising that she had not

damaged her wings. Fortunately the water only trickled through the grid, so she had been in no danger of drowning; had we not found her, though, she would most likely have starved to death. Probably the cock bird had called when he came back and perhaps she had answered, and her calls had been overridden by the splashing of the water.

We removed her carefully and examined her. She did not struggle. No legs were broken, the wings were undamaged but she was wet and hungry. She seemed rather dazed. Having never handled an adult king-fisher before we were surprised how light she was, and how much more of her was feathers than appeared. We dried her in our handkerchiefs and warmed her in our hands. When she seemed a little drier we put her on one of the perches and retreated into the hide to watch her next actions.

First she preened all over and sat fluttering and drooping her wings, trying to dry them. She must have been terribly hungry, for she soon dived in to catch a fish. Her perch was very near the water, so not much effort was involved. But her feathers were already waterlogged and the water barely released her. She struggled ashore on foot. There were stones at the side of the pool which she climbed up, and she sat on the edge of the pool drying herself. Unfortunately she had lost the fish in the fray. Eventually after twenty minutes she made her way on to the perch, and it was another twenty minutes before she attempted to fish again. Then she caught a fish and ate it, still looking wet and bedraggled. It was 9 o'clock and near dusk. We decided that it might have been a better idea to have taken her home and dried her with a hair-drier.

She was not frightened away when we reappeared from the hide and stood debating which was the best way to catch her. It was some minutes before we decided on our approach and as we moved in closer she flew off. We watched her disappear into the trees and waited in the hope of seeing her again. We hoped that she had not eventually grounded. It was too dark to watch any more or even to go looking for her. We gave the nestlings a further fish apiece before leaving rather reluctantly, planning to return early next morning. We were very anxious for the hen's condition and by 6 o'clock next morning had stationed ourselves in the hide to see if she was still alive.

The cock was feeding the young. Each time he appeared we hoped it would be her and our spirits dampened when we saw the all-black beak of the cock. Each time he came, he called, and each time did not receive an answer. Sometimes he even came back without a fish and called. All day long there was no sign of her and by evening we had given up all hope.

A sedge warbler came down to the perch. It, too, was searching for food for a hungry brood. It flew to the bank and clung on to a root, innocently picking things over, unaware it was so close to the nest. Too close. Suddenly a blue form swooped down, mobbing it. It was the hen. She must have been watching from nearby.

She was beautiful, no longer the poor, miserable, bedraggled creature of the previous evening, but a fine, brilliant, well-preened bird. She fished fearlessly only three or four inches from the place in which she had been trapped, and even sat on the baffleboard to kill the fish. She had more sense than to drop it behind this time, but if she had it would no longer have been dangerous, for the space was now blocked with rags and other cloths and there was a board covering it.

After two days' absence from her parental duties, she had not lost her instinct and went on to feed her young. They were successfully launched into the world on the 23rd day.

9

Fledging

WE NEVER discovered what first prompts a young king-fisher to leave the safety of the nest chamber and to venture down the dark tunnel to the bright world out-side. At first we thought that starvation forced the youngsters out. In some cases, especially when they were some distance from water, the parents ceased to feed the brood the day before. Certainly this happened to the brood in the chalk pit. On the previous evening the hen, who had been looking after the brood by her-self, was joined by her mate. This was in fact the first time we had seen him, and for some minutes they flew excitedly round the pit. This is a common occurrence when a pair meet after a long absence. The cock bird settled in a clump of ivy at the top of the chalk cliff opposite the nest. He sat there making a raucous noise, screaming and chirping, then took short flights about the pit, always passing before the nest as he did so. This sort of behaviour lasted for about an hour and a half, and the youngsters were not fed again that even-ing.

We thought that this might be the calling-out of the

young after they had been fed very little, and we anxiously awaited their appearance at the nest entrance. We were quite aware of the situation. In such a poor evening light we would be unable to film them leaving the nest, and we hoped for the film's sake that they would not leave that evening. It was soon dark, and still nothing happened. The parents had disappeared, no doubt to catch a last fish before going to roost. We were convinced, though, that the two youngsters would leave early next morning, and by 5.30 a.m. we were in position, with the camera set up opposite the nest hole. At 6 the first youngster flew out of the nest and was shortly followed by his nest mate. As yet there was no sign of their parents. The first bird gained height and flew into a beech tree, one of many which screen the pit from the road. The other bird, who was not so strong, landed on the ground not far from us. By half-past seven the hen bird had arrived on the scene and was feeding the youngster who was still in the beech tree. The other was still too weak to fly very far, and thinking that a few fish might help, we caught some and fed it. Soon it too was sitting in the beech tree and by mid-day they were both gone. We hoped that they had found their way to the river.

In the case of our own kingfishers the youngsters left of their own accord. The parents did not stop feeding them, but went on till eventually they were taking fish into an empty nest. When this finally happened the parent flew off with the fish and presumably searched for a youngster to feed. Of the second brood we saw very little after the first day. On the first evening out one youngster was fishing below the old mill but after that most of the brood seemed to have disappeared. Either they moved out of the territory or they perished.

The third brood left at intervals but eventually all met up and sat together in the trees, in various places at heights from 10 to 20 feet, up and down the main river. It would have been virtually impossible for us to have spotted them had we not been familiar with their new call, a single chirp, and seen them bobbing in the bushes, for their colouring merged imperceptibly with their surroundings. They seemed to have little idea that fish were their food or that fish were to be found in the river beneath them. Most of the time they sat looking up into the sky instead of training their eyes in a kingfisher-like attitude on the water.

One member of the third brood was sitting alone on his first evening out over one of the most dangerous stretches of the river. Just behind the old corn mill there are deep whirlpools and eddying currents formed by the water rushing madly through the hatches of the mill. There, sitting peacefully on an overhanging branch, was one of the newly-fledged kingfishers, a small blue spark in the shadows of the mill. Two hours before it had been safe in the nest; now it was preparing to throw its life away in the swift-moving current. We held our breaths as we watched it dive into the mill pool, and expected that it would be gone for ever. The water must have been seven feet deep, and the current was strong. But the little bird emerged and just managed to find enough energy to release itself from the water. Throwing itself into the water so soon after leaving the nest was a great feat of courage for the little bird; dusk was drawing near and it was probably hungry. Then it flew across the river and perched on some hurdles. Here the current was more subdued. Once again it dived. Catching nothing, it soon flew off in the dusk towards the cressbeds where it might just have had time to find one of the hundreds of thousands of sticklebacks resident there. By now it was too late for us to follow the bird and expect to see it fish again that evening, and if we had done so we might have disturbed it and ruined its chances of catching a fish that night.

For two or three days after the birds had left the nest the parents became conscious of their duty towards their inexperienced offspring and spent much of the day flying up and down stream, usually fairly high, with a silver fish in their beaks. After a few days the youngsters can fish well enough to survive on their own and no longer utter the single chirp by which the parents find them. If the youngster survives the dangers of the main river and then goes on to find the safer shallow streams, it has usually learnt the proper technique and the easiest places from which to fish. But it still has dangers to overcome. If its aim is not good and if it has to dive too many times before being successful it may get impatient and instead of waiting to dry its feathers off sufficiently before the next dive it may get waterlogged, in which case the final dive is disastrous and the current will carry the bird away. A week after fledging it is rare to find more than half of the brood still alive. Those that have survived stick fairly close together and fish in the same places. This behaviour creates a problem later but for the time being they are happy. But once the territorial streak is aroused and the parents begin to drive them this aggressive behaviour catches on. Soon the young turn against each

The master fisherman surveys his kingdom

A juvenile kingfisher prepares to beat a stickleback against
the perch. Only when the fish is dead will its spines flatten

A spectacle to daunt any bird: our first piece of underwater photographic apparatus, in the form of an old enamel lightshade about a foot deep, partially cemented with gravel and standing on a tin box in the stream. The camera looked up at the fish through a perspex porthole to the side and near the bottom. A cable release leads to the hide

other and begin to guard for themselves a favourite
fishing perch. No longer do they want to share fishing
haunts, and they prove it with aggressive displays.

One such display occurred at a new set we had constructed especially to denote autumn. It consisted of a
small pool of sticklebacks with a screen of weeping
autumnal willows. By the 28th of August a young
kingfisher in the last stages of the moult claimed the
pool for himself. When one of his brothers arrived
expecting to be allowed to fish the new owner turned
aggressive. After several vertical and horizontal display patterns the new owner chased the intruder out.

Next day the owner was sitting in the yellow willow
leaves, preening peacefully in the sun. It was nibbling
along the inside of its wing with the tip of its beak
when it suddenly sat bolt upright, head pointing sky-
wards and wings drooping, and began to move its beak
in a slow and exaggerated fashion. The other bird in a
nearby bush displayed differently, lying along the
branch, horizontally flattened. I think that this was
more of a fright display, for the cock bird had done the
same one day when he heard some fishermen approaching the stream. After the display a chase once again
ensued and the owner returned some minutes later,
panting, and continued to fish. But he had not reckoned with his parents' intrusion, for the pool was still
part of their territory. Since the end of the nesting
season the parents had visited the stream very rarely,
for they spent most of their time fishing in the cressbeds. Now, with autumn approaching and the possible
threat of a hard winter's fishing, those little beaks that
were at present digging into precious reserves would
have to go. In early September the cock bird returned

to his part of the territory. He was in full moult. His original bright colours were mottled and patchy where feathers were missing. Altogether he looked rather moth-eaten, even too rough-looking for us to bother about filming him.

Even so he was standing no nonsense with his interfering offspring. Each time they appeared at the pool he chased them away. We had always noticed how noisy it is on the river in autumn and now we understood why. The kingfisher chasing-out season was in full swing, and kingfishers could be heard calling at almost any time of the day. There was no peace for any kingfisher to settle down to fishing. This sort of behaviour lasts for several weeks. The cock and the hen have different fishing territories within their single overall territory, but nevertheless take any opportunity of encroaching upon their mate's fishing rights.

One day in particular, the hen was fishing upstream, a little farther than she should have been, in the cock's territory. (The cock was probably resting somewhere else.) We were watching the particular part of the hen's territory which was normally her central point. Suddenly a youngster flew upstream, calling, and landed upon her favourite perch. Hearing this call the hen came back downstream and on spotting the bird flew towards it uttering her anger note, an aggressive guttural 'shrit-it-it.' The youngster flew off in the direction he had come only a few minutes previously, and she followed close behind. All was quiet for a while and then the hen reappeared and landed on the perch. After shaking herself and readjusting a few feathers she flew off upstream again to purloin a few more of her mate's fish. She had not been gone long before the cheeky youngster reappeared, but this time, having learnt his lesson, he did not call, and remained fishing quietly for some time. But then there was a commotion. Flying downstream at a fair rate came the hen bird, closely pursued by her mate. She must have exceeded her territorial limits. Now again she saw the youngster, who took to wing ahead of the other two, and all three disappeared downstream. The hen reappeared and this time stayed to fish her own stream; the cock returned upstream after flying around the rest of the cressbeds, and the youngster must have sought out a new territory, for it did not reappear again. Eventually all the remaining young moved away and the side-stream resumed its original quietude.

For two or three more weeks during that September, the old birds continued to moult. Every day we would find a tail- or wing-feather, or a bright azure back-feather and a dull orange one. By now the young must have been far away. There were many new places to visit: lakes, canals, rivers, reservoirs, gravel-pits, and, best of all, goldfish ponds. The latter in particular must be a relief for the young kingfisher: big fish in a confined area, easy prey. One goldfish pond nearby contained about 140 fish at one time but the owner, who fed the fish every morning, began to notice a steady decline in numbers. Each day a few more disappeared without explanation or trace. Eventually, on rising earlier one morning he discovered the culprit. A kingfisher was sitting on the pond's edge with a newly-caught goldfish in his beak. He did not fish there during the day as one might expect, but only came in the very early mornings.

We had tried for a long time to film our kingfishers

taking goldfish and we had even built a goldfish pond over by the river for the purpose. But for some reason they did not take the fish, even though they were the right size, two to three inches long. We decided that perhaps the colour put them off and we bought the brown variety for them to try. These they took, and gradually we put the gold ones back. For some reason the birds still would not take them. There was no evidence on the fish that the kingfisher had even tried to catch them, for a fish caught and dropped by a king-fisher will usually bear the bird's beak-mark on one side of its body.

IO

Autumn

ALTHOUGH there is no evidence of the overseas migration of the kingfisher in autumn, there have been occasions when they have been reported from a coastline, and there is definitely a general southerly movement of some birds. For instance some kingfishers in Scotland apparently move south. In the September of 1914 and the August of 1935 parties of kingfishers amounting to thirty-five birds were seen at the Isle of May and at the mouth of the Tay, flying out to sea in a south-easterly direction. In one British Ornithological Club migration report, there is a reference to a small passage of kingfishers at Langstone Harbour (Hampshire) in 1911, the numbers varying up to eight daily from day to day throughout September to mid-October. This, together with lightship reports of kingfishers being picked up dead, is evidence of a decided movement of birds leaving inland summer resorts for coastal areas in autumn, and their return in the spring.[1]

[1] *a* Kingfisher reported dead on Blackwater Bank Lightship (Ireland) July, 1904.

During passage, kingfishers are still aggressive whilst fishing, though by and large they do not fight. There is, however, a variety of displays to be seen, the general object being to drive the intruder away from a newly formed fishing territory. One paper records two kingfishers on River Erme, South Devon, actually sitting on the ground facing one another, and many varying types of displays followed. Firstly the birds flew backwards and forwards exchanging positions. Their sitting attitude towards each other was a penguin-like upright stance with drooping wings; they never sat more than three feet apart. Then they slowly bowed down towards each other, keeping their heads and bodies in a straight line, always returning to the upright stance. Every action was slow and deliberate. Sometimes the bow was very forward with the beak half-opened, and appearing to touch the ground. Then, with bodies in a crouched position, the birds sat fanning their wings. The spreading or flicking of wings, a movement stimulated by some action on the other's part, appeared to be a threat. Occasionally there was a sandpiper-like bobbing of the tail. There was also an upright stretching of the neck and pointing of the bill, done in rather an exaggerated fashion, and on one or

---

b Kingfisher reported dead on Bull Rock Lighthouse (Ireland) September, 1904.

c Kingfisher reported dead on Leman and Ower Lightship (Norfolk) October, 1909.

d Kingfisher reported dead on Kentish Knock Lightship, March, 1904.

e Kingfisher reported dead Orfordness Lighthouse (Suffolk), March, 1884, with another mainland record of the same date.

two occasions the birds actually came together and touched bills in slow motion. On two occasions the birds became very excited calling a rapid aggressive 'shrit-it-it,' and after twenty-five minutes of continual display the birds merely sat and faced each other, before flying off upstream. As no observations were made upon the colour of the two birds' beaks, the only distinguishing factor between the sexes, it is hard to say whether the two birds were male and female, trying to form a pair bond, or two males displaying aggressiveness over a fishing territory.

When the kingfishers became so enraged over each other's presence as to reach fighting pitch, the end result for the weaker bird is a ducking in the water. There are records of this type of display on migration routes abroad. In France, the kingfishers, en route to some warmer place, remain in the Inner Geneva Basin for several days to rest. Usually they prefer the quiet waters on the edge of the jetty near the breakwaters. Here two kingfishers were once seen beginning their fight by opening and closing their beaks excitedly. Then they flapped their wings at each other, and after a short while one flew at the other and perched upon the back of the weaker one, who tried to get away but only succeeded in being dragged into the water. The aggressor had a hold upon its beak and was trying to drown it. The weaker one managed to get away and flew to the perch near the breakwater. But its aggressor was not going to let it rest there. He attacked again and the two birds went zig-zagging across the water. All through the fight another kingfisher sat watching only fifteen yards away, apparently uninterested and completely aloof.

During the October of 1964, we saw very little of the kingfishers at the stream, although we heard them call in the cressbeds. We decided to attract them back to the stream, which was by then a little neglected. After we had cleaned the stream up, we caught some bullheads, having spent some time finding them, and placed them in the old tin bath beneath a perch. The birds did not return immediately, and we had to wait several days for their reappearance. At the beginning of November they both appeared, together again. They were brilliantly coloured and within a few hours had eaten all the fish we had put in the bath. Thereafter we had to keep the bath regularly supplied.

With the birds back again we decided to try another experiment. With the aid of a stuffed kingfisher we wanted to find out our kingfisher's reaction to an intruder in its territory at this time of the year. For this purpose we had been given a somewhat discoloured specimen, with one eye and broken legs, which would nevertheless be sufficient for the job. Its back at least was the correct brilliant azure. We set it up on a mossy log in the stream and retired to the hide to film any reactions.

It was a quiet day, as the passing days of autumn are. The trout-fishing season had long since ended and there was no one on the river banks. Most of the migrant birds had gone too and the river was a somewhat quieter place without them. Only the occasional sharp note of the coot broke the silence and somewhere nearby a moorhen clucked. Pied and grey wagtails were active near the old mill. The wind swayed the dead vegetation that had in the summer been a tangled mass of bloom. A party of goldfinches swung upon the seeding thistles near the hide. Drupes of berries, red and purple, draped across the fading hedges, and in the still pool and the ditches the yellow sycamore leaves, marred with large black dots, mingled with the slim leaves of the willows and the beaten gold of the horse chestnut. Beneath this covering of leaves sticklebacks were visible from time to time.

We had been in the hide for about twenty minutes before anything happened. Soon a blue form could be seen winging its way towards us. The cock kingfisher, looking as magnificent as ever, alighted upon the perch near the mossy log, and on seeing another kingfisher there, called in the usually friendly tones with which he greets his mate. There was no reply. He moved uncomfortably upon his perch. This was not his hen or she would have replied. The breeze suddenly caught the stuffed bird and moved it slightly. This must be an intruder, the last straw after the two birds had spent weeks ridding themselves of their own offspring.

The cock bird drooped his wings and sat bolt upright, with his beak moving slowly in aggressive reaction. He called again, this time using his aggressive note 'shrit-it-it-it.' Still there was no answer, only another slight movement of the stuffed bird in the breeze. This was too much for him. He took immediate advantage of the situation and jumped off his perch to land upon the stuffed bird's back. Fortunately we had had the foresight to anchor the bird firmly upon the log, and it now remained upright. We had thought, however, that a longer display time would have elapsed before the cock took action; even a robin will display dramatically for some time before actually attacking the intruder. And attacking was what the kingfisher was now engaged in. With one foot on the back of the stuffed bird's neck and the other around its beak, it was pecking hard into the side of its neck. Some five minutes later it stopped, still in the same position, for a rest and looked around, perhaps to see if its mate was about. Refreshed it then continued its pecking. The stuffed bird began to sway and soon toppled over, falling off the log and into the stream where it became lodged in a shallow pool. (This time of the year the water was so shallow in the stream that the gravelly bed protruded in many places.) The kingfisher, who had returned to his perch, was still not sure if he had won the fight and pounced down upon his victim, which now lay on its side, and, standing upon it, once more began to peck it. After several minutes he seemed to lose interest. Having calmed down he returned to his perch, still looking at the stuffed bird, and then flew off in the direction of the cressbeds.

Normally the object of a fight between two kingfishers is a territorial one; the owner of a territory aims to drive out, or possibly drown, its opponent—or at least to give it a ducking. Certainly the sight of this silent intruder had angered the cock bird to the point of fighting, and it had with some difficulty managed to get its victim into the water, although the shallowness prevented it ducking or drowning it there.

We did not try the experiment again as it seemed that there was little else to learn now that we had already proved the kingfisher to be possibly territorial even to a stuffed colleague.

11

Winter

So FAR we had seen the kingfisher and the river in their most attractive and charming settings. The blossom of the pussy willow and the glories of the autumn berries made some of the best backgrounds for our beautiful actors. Winter was approaching now, with the promise of many a bleak and dreary day and, too, the dreariest of all background settings. The snow now would make the only pleasant pictorial framework for any filming. When the last golden leaf had drifted away downstream the wind rustled through the pale grass stalks, cracking and bending them until only a flattened mass remained.

For most of the winter the river is very quiet. With the departure of the summer visitors, the only residents there are the local birds, a few passing wintering birds, the waterkeeper Mac, his dog, and us. It is a desolate home now for the moorhen and the coot, though the river does provide some shelter for them. Through the morning mist of the river the trill of the dabchicks was still audible. The mallard were already beginning to form pairs. They frequent the very quiet part of the river where the weeping willows and laurels give them some cover, for now that the shooting season is open they are more wary than ever and take flight at the first sign of disturbance. We watched them through the tall reed screen, which still offers us a little cover. The ducks up-end themselves in their curious search for food. Further upstream, where a small brook runs parallel to the river behind a hedge, we may chance to find some smaller duck, the teal.

The tall alders may be bare of leaves but not of bird life. The tree-tops are a twittering mass of small birds. The winter visitors, the siskins and redpolls, have joined the great tits searching the cones of the alders seeding catkins, before the seeds are shaken out by the wind.

The reedy bank of the river is no longer bright. As far as the eye can see the pale ochre of the dead vegetation merges with the slopes of the stubble field. But even in these dead reeds of the riverside some wild life remains; the mouse-like wren creeps in and out of the stems in search of any remaining insects.

The frosty morning transforms the riverside to some of its former beauty. The skeleton frame of the parsley once again flowers, this time with a sparkling layer of frost. The lapwing is driven from the hard-ploughed fields to the riverside water-meadows and the cress-beds, where aquatic insects can be found in abundance even on a frosty morning. Here, with the greenshank, three of these birds always winter; here, with some snipe, they can search undisturbed the beds that are being replanted with cress. Starlings in flocks come to forage too, and under cover of night mallard drop in in the same furtive way as they used to drop into the barley fields in autumn, and do a lot of damage to the newly planted cress.

Beneath the grey sheet of water which is the river, at times whipped into sparkling crests by the wind, the trout lie. They eat little during the winter; all summer long they have gorged themselves upon countless flies and nymphs, but now they are lean with spawning and seem tired of life, though their appetite is aroused when Mac the waterkeeper comes upstream with a bucketful of fish pellets for them. For the kingfisher the going is not hard as long as he can fish all day, though a cold spell can mean disaster. The water can freeze over and lock away his larder, although this seldom occurs in places such as the cressbeds, which are fed from springs.

There is a record in *British Birds* of a kingfisher trapped by frost. The accident occurred one frosty morning in December, 1961, at Mill Hill Golf Links in Middlesex. A kingfisher was found stuck by frost to a narrow iron pipe overhanging the water. It hung by its left leg, which in its struggles it had broken in two places. It was unable to free itself. The adhesive quality of frost is well-known and the bird may have only been perched there a short while since it is unlikely to have roosted there. Although it was cared for and fed, it died within two days.

We waited for the snow to come so that we could film the kingfisher in its winter setting. We kept the bath in the stream well stocked with sticklebacks so that we could be sure that when the snow did come we would not have a hard job looking for the actor. At least one of the birds still came daily to the stream. They did not fish together now; both had their own favourite perches in different parts of the territory.

The first snow of the winter came. It was not much, but the cold wind made it an ordeal rather than a pleasure to sit in the hide and wait for the kingfisher to turn up. It became so cold, with a gale howling round the wooden hide, that we were eventually forced to light a small paraffin stove to keep warm enough to operate the camera. Unfortunately this had the effect of steaming up the lenses every time we lit it, so when the bird eventually turned up we had to freeze again. There was no whistle as the familiar blue streak hurtled down towards the hide. The kingfisher sat huddled up in the bitter wind upon the perch. It was the cock bird, and he proceeded to watch the sticklebacks swimming around in the bath. These fish must have been the easiest he caught during the winter, for they could not escape or hide from him as they did in the cressbeds and streams. And we thought how conspicuous he was now to any predator against such a white background, though fortunately for the kingfisher there are only a few hawks in these parts nowadays. Unless the snow became very deep and the streams froze our kingfisher would be safe from the hazards of winter, though in the hard winter of 1962/3, it was not an uncommon occurrence for the waterkeepers on the Test to pick up the frozen bodies of kingfishers. This sudden snow shower was not a hazard to our birds for as soon as we had finished taking our shots it stopped snowing and began to thaw. To illustrate a kingfisher dead in the snow we laid out the stuffed one while it was still snowing and filmed it on the way back home.

We felt it would be very unlikely that we would ever find a real one dead in the snow—we hoped not anyway!

But severe winters are a testing time for the kingfisher population and can drastically reduce their numbers. Once their food sources freeze they have to move to the estuaries, seeking a complete change of diet in the form of shrimps and crustaceans. In northern Europe the kingfishers move south early, before the rivers freeze. In Germany the bird is known as the ice bird for it always moves out before the ice moves in. They travel to the warmer southern coastlines and suitable localities like Majorca.

In Britain the kingfisher does not travel so far, mostly only to the river estuaries. The most northerly ones move down to the east coast, often in numbers. The autumn dispersal of the young left our particular pair in the more temperate climes of the River Test, with a food supply which had only to be shared between themselves throughout the winter. Should this dwindle they may have had at times to visit places like goldfish ponds and perhaps, if they could get in, trout hatcheries!

On the Fens and Broads the shallow pools are always the first to freeze and the birds have to move to inland dykes and then to the coast. Severe winters cutting off the kingfishers' food supplies drive the birds to take food types that are not a normal part of their winter diets. In the hard winter of 1859/60, one Norfolk kingfisher was seen pitching close to the bank of a stream trying to catch something. Then, having caught it, it retired to the handrail of a bridge and tried to swallow it. Suddenly it fell over backwards and the observers picked it up dead. On examination it was found to have attempted to swallow a shrew, which was the cause of its untimely end. The bird must indeed have been hard-pressed for food.

Yet another kingfisher went farther afield. It was seen taking suet from a bird-table at Smallburgh Rectory in Hickling. On another occasion a Devon kingfisher did the same thing but the housewife, who saw it happening, was cleaning some herring at the time and thought the bird might like the titbits. It readily took these and for several days slices of fish were taken from the bird-table by the hungry king-fisher.

Very severe winters, when total freezing of the rivers occurs, take a large toll of the kingfisher population. In 1889, the cold spell produced a long period of skating weather in January. Near Newbury, on the Kennet in Berkshire, frozen kingfishers were picked up daily along the banks and in the adjacent fields.

The high mortality was particularly noted in the hard winter of 1939/40, when the Thames was frozen over. In 1934 there had been a count of the kingfisher population along sixty-eight miles of the Thames, and the average number of birds was 1.8 per mile. The 1939/40 winter drastically reduced the population to one or two pairs along that sixty-eight miles. Thereafter a careful account was kept of the increasing population. It was noted that within three years their numbers were nearly back to normal.

It was the winter of 1962/3 that noticeably reduced the kingfisher population, hitting this species harder than any other. In addition to the fresh waters being frozen the kingfishers that had time enough to reach the estuaries found these frozen over as well, and it was only in Dorset and here in Hampshire that the population remained normal.

12

Enemies of the Kingfisher

Nowadays the kingfisher population is affected more
by the weather than by the human element, but
during the nineteenth century man persecuted the
kingfisher for so many reasons that, had not the Wild
Bird Protection Act 1880 put an end to the ruthless
slaughter (although it only protected the bird for the
close season), the kingfisher in England might have
been extinct to-day.

Field investigation at the beginning of the century
revealed that the nesting sites had badly decreased
in Cumberland, Cheshire, Devon, Herefordshire,
Leicestershire, Middlesex, Warwickshire, Worcester-
shire, and Yorkshire. There were several reasons for
the decline, all as bad as each other: personal gain,
decoration, or adornment, and, worse still, sheer pointless brutality.

The severe 1859/60 winter involved a natural
slaughter, from which the surviving numbers could
recover if left on their own, without the unforeseen
menace of the fashion trade and fish culture. One
would have thought that so beautiful a bird would,

alive, be an object of admiration to all. Not so. The Victorians preferred them dead and stuffed, elegant ornaments for their drawing-rooms. Of course it was not only the kingfisher that suffered. The more recently discovered foreign birds were set up in fantastic arrays, and the demand for some of our own started a decline in many species. Such was the slaughter of the kingfisher that one bird-stuffer in Norfolk had a hundred skins sent to him in one year. The method used to catch the birds undamaged was to put a snare or net across the nest hole to catch the adults, leaving the young to starve or the eggs to rot.

It was not only for furnishing ornaments that the Victorians wanted the kingfisher, but also for female fashion. It probably never occurred to the owners of those evil hats that the adoption of one particular feather or fur may have been the death warrant of a species. F. Buckland, writing in *The Field*, on 26th March, 1864, said that on the previous Saturday he met a man on the Thames whose special mission was to shoot as many kingfishers as he could. These then went to London to be made into ornaments for ladies' hats.

If this section of the community had only a small influence upon the kingfisher's economic status, there was one other which had a much more powerful and severe bearing: the pisciculturists. These assumed that the kingfisher took too many trout and salmon fry, and so condemned it out of hand. Once a bird has been given a bad name it is hard to clear it, and there seemed no end to its persecution. For the few trout they may have taken they paid a very heavy penalty. But the accusation was founded entirely upon false information, as anyone carrying out a scientific investigation into their food supply might have found out.

In fact they probably do fish stock more good than harm for there is no other species that removes so many enemies of game fish ova as the kingfisher. It was not until 1921 that Dr. Walter E. Collinge pointed out the facts and probably saved the bird from extinction. Kingfishers were shot or trapped unmercifully. One method of catching the bird was to set a pole trap on a stump, upon which the unwary birds alighted. This clumsy contraption was one of the cruellest of traps, for it seldom killed the bird outright but merely held it while crushing its legs. The bird would hang there till it died of agony or hunger. In this manner, says one author, as many as fifteen birds were caught in one week during the autumn at the turn of the century. Then, as if the fisherman had not taken his persecution far enough, he set to exploring the banksides during the spring and summer and blocking up the kingfishers' nesting holes with stones. To insult the birds yet further he used their feathers to tie his fishing flies.

To-day the educated pisciculturist has more enlightened and humane views. It is natural for birds and animals to flock to areas which provide better or more abundant food. Kingfishers are no different, given a daily food supply that is never failing, like our kingfisher bird table or, more commonly, a trout hatchery. Far-sighted hatchery owners now prevent the kingfisher from getting into the hatchery by wiring in the 'stews' or breeding ponds with mesh too small for the kingfisher to squeeze through. At one such hatchery the owner has no objection to the kingfisher's presence; indeed he watches the bird quite happily as it sits on the outlet pipe from the hatchery waiting to catch the sickly trout which are doomed to die as they are turned out daily into a gutter.

Kingfishers were caught even in the first three decades of this century. Along the East Coast nets were stretched across the beaches to entangle the wild-fowl. Although the 4-inch mesh was diagonally stretched it was too small for the kingfisher to dart through, and so it became entangled. The shore shooters would collect a shilling apiece for their skins. No doubt kingfishers are still trapped to-day by a few ignorant individuals, despite total protection of the species by the law under the Protection of Birds Act 1954.

A factor in the decline of the kingfisher population is the reduction of the available number of territories through pollution. In the Midlands and the North, where many streams have been polluted with industrial effluent and probably also with pesticides, and where the life cycle of the river has been gradually reduced, the death or permanent evacuation of various species from certain areas has inevitably followed.

Natural predators are relatively few. In our type of area where the river runs through the villages, the king-fishers' worst enemy is the cat. One kingfisher of the first pair we started to watch was caught by a cat, and the whole breeding cycle for the bird in this area was curtailed for a year, until it had found a new mate. Apparently, though, the kingfisher, among other brightly coloured birds, has distasteful flesh and predators do not prefer it.

The brown rat is the only animal who does not care

what its next meal might be. The hen kingfisher of our
story was only four years old when she met her terrible
fate, early in 1967. She was brooding her newly
hatched youngsters when a rat dug down into the back
of the nest. We only found a few blue feathers mingled
with some orange ones, part of her skull, and her
lower mandible, and nothing of the young remained at
all. The rat had gorged himself on the whole lot. It
was a sad end for a bird who had worked so hard, but
this is the rule of Nature: eat and be eaten. Nature may
be compellingly beautiful but it is also incomparably
cruel.

13

Kingfisher Song

THE KINGFISHER is not musically inclined. Indeed the most sombrely-clad warbler can outdo it in song. The main call is 'Chee-ee, chee-ee' and is adapted for many uses. Most usually the call is an advertisement note as it travels around its territory.

All birdsong can be grouped into three major sections, according to reproductive, social, and individual functions. The kingfisher's calls clearly have several functions. He must primarily make it known that he is the owner of a particular territory; he must identify himself to his mate, and strengthen their pair bond; there must be a call to stimulate sexual behaviour, and another to signal changes in domestic duties; and there must be one to intimidate and drive out competitors.

The kingfisher is constantly advertising its presence and therefore its ownership of territory. Almost every time it flies from perch to perch as it journeys around its territory, it calls, once or twice, usually just before landing. If its mate is anywhere nearby it will always answer with the same call, and all is presumed to be well.

With the advance of the breeding season, the king-fishers chase each other round the territory and call excitedly nearly all the time. The 'chee-ee' is repeated more rapidly and when they get down to fishing together, or maybe start to excavate, the calls are so rapidly uttered alternately by both birds that the listener might get the impression that there is only one bird calling.

Once the nest excavation has begun there is a change of call note. When the initial depression has been made and one bird is actually in the tunnel, perhaps out of sight of the other, the birds take on a quieter, more serious attitude. To assure its mate that all is well and that there are no intruders about, the non-digging bird, usually perched outside the nest, will call softly from time to time—a very low 'chee, chee, chee.' But if any danger approaches, it calls sharply to the digger to fly off.

Once the nest is complete the soft 'chee, chee' will be used by the hen, but becomes louder and more appealing. She takes an upright stance, bill pointing upwards, wings loosely hung and juddering. This stimulates the cock bird, who immediately goes off and catches a fish, returns and feeds her, and then usually treads her.

As soon as incubation has begun silence reigns. Only at change-over time will the non-sitting bird come down and call its mate off the nest. They usually exchange a few brief, sometimes excited syllables before one disappears off to fish and the other to take its turn upon the eggs. Once the young have hatched out brooding and feeding have to be carried out. It is necessary for the bird arriving with the fish to call the other off the nest; this is to ensure a clear passage in the nest as the tunnel is only big enough for one bird to use at a time.

The young kingfishers themselves make a fearful noise when hungry: a soft purring, rather grasshopper-like noise which increases in volume as they increase in size. When a parent approaches with food, he or she croaks to attract their attention, and immediately the whole company, or at least those that are hungriest, start to call. When the young are ready to fly they drop this purring note for a single chirp, which they retain until they have learnt to feed independently for themselves. This chirp enables the searching adult to find and feed them. The anger note of the kingfisher is a guttural 'Shrit-it-it-it,' emitted continuously to drive away intruding kingfishers. The kingfisher has also made the same noise when we have disturbed it fishing. The kingfisher does not have much of a vocabulary, but then with such a vivid plumage it does not need to advertise its presence like other birds.

14

Hand-rearing

In 1862 a Norfolk bird-stuffer kept four young kingfishers who had been taken from their nest. They lived
in a small aviary which was large enough for them to
display their natural habits, and they looked after
themselves by fishing from a bowl of minnows in their
cage. After eating the fish that they had caught for
themselves they would try and steal one from their
neighbour by dragging each other along the perch till
eventually they succeeded in tearing the fish in half.

During the nineteenth century, when snares were
put across nest holes to catch the parent birds, many
families of young kingfishers were left to starve. One
such abandoned family was taken to the London Zoo
where they were reared by a foster-kingfisher of the
same species till they were of a reasonable age. Then
for no apparent reason the foster-bird killed them all
by spearing them with its beak. Possibly they had
arrived at the age when they were taking the foster-
parent's food and the foster-parent reacted instinc-
tively to remove any competing kingfisher from its
territory. This tragic situation might have been
avoided if the young kingfishers had been given a

place of their own in which to fish, or if they had been released.

A more successful hand-rearing story comes from the records of a hatchery owner who lived on the Test. When he saw that the parent kingfishers were bringing minnows, roach, but also pike to their nest in a gravel pit he realised that the birds could do some good in a trout stream. He was amazed how quickly the parents fed their young, for they would take seven fish in ten minutes.

When the young were about to fly he dug down into the nest, having first taken the precaution of blocking the tunnel to prevent them escaping. He took the seven young and succeeded in rearing four of them in a wicker basket. They ate minnows and pieces of pike which he put down their throats. When they were fully-grown, they ate twelve minnows a day each. Later three of them came to grief when he put them into a large cage which was half darkened. The sole survivor lived happily through the winter but escaped in the spring whilst being fed. The owner could not catch it though it remained friendly and fairly tame and followed him about, living on the river near the house. It would not take minnows from his hand but when he put them on a handrail and stepped back two yards it would come down for them. In his garden there was a large hawthorn and this was the bird's favourite resting place. It lived there for a while and the wild kingfishers would join it.

In 1965, our pair of kingfishers returned and nested in their old bank. Although we did not need to film them we still kept a watch on them. It was quite easy for they were nesting in the first hole of the previous year, which they had cleaned out, and soon started to lay a clutch of eggs. We did not look into the nest after they had started laying but we knew from the parents' actions that they had started to incubate. A month later we decided to look in at the brood for we estimated that the youngsters must be a week old. We were curious to find out what the clutch size had been. On the 11th May we opened up the back of the nest and could scarcely believe the sight in front of us.

There was a collapsed heap of bodies in the middle of the chamber, naked, blind and completely helpless as they lay on their stomachs. We took them out carefully one by one. There were six still alive and the seventh was dead. Their bodies were already chill and they were in a state of exhaustion. Once again the kingfishers' first brood was about to fail. There was very little time left. It was obvious that their parents were no longer caring for them, so we might as well try to save them if we could. There was not so much as a chirp left in their weak bodies. I wrapped them up carefully in my woollen jacket and ran home. Whilst they sat in the jumper before an electric fire Ron was busy catching some fish. After a time the warmth of the fire began to revive them, and although they were still too weak to stand, they chirped quietly. Half an hour later, after a meal of sticklebacks, they were just able to stand again. We kept them near the fire all that night, and we had to feed them at two-hourly intervals. They chirped incessantly so long and so loud that we could not sleep for the noise. There was no doubt at all that they were on the road to recovery.

They soon looked healthy and grew very fast. Until they were all feathered the electric fire was left on to keep them warm. We wondered why the parents had deserted them. There was no sign of any intruder or predator at the nest. Maybe the youngsters, weakened by the cold they had experienced whilst the parents were too long gone from the nest, were unable to ask for food when presented with it. Therefore the parent, assuming that its mate had satisfied the little birds' hunger, retired to the perch outside and ate the fish itself. We had proved the previous year that, when one bird was able to get easy fishing and could feed the whole brood in five minutes, the other bird, on finding that the youngsters would take no more food for a while, would eat the fish itself.

The youngsters lived in a cardboard box which was half-filled with dry earth and had a depression at one end. This was the nearest way we could simulate the actual nest. We found that they would all huddle together quite naturally as they had done in their own nest. With a book covering the box except for the far end, which let in a little light as the nest hole would have done, the birds were not far off living in normal conditions. The light entering at one end was a necessity, as it enabled them to keep their excrement, which is always aimed in the direction of the light, away from themselves. Had it been totally dark they might have fouled the chamber in which they lived and defiled each other. We thought that these more natural conditions might be important to their development.

The fish we gave to the youngsters amounted to about fifty a day, and feeding times were always exciting. At first we fed them at two-hourly intervals, but after the first week-end we had to go back to work, and this meant that their feeding times would have to be changed. So we fed them at 6 in the morning, then at about 8.45 before we left for work. By the time we had travelled home again at lunchtime it was 12.45 p.m. and the young birds were calling ravenously. They had another feed about 1.20 p.m., which had to last them until 5.30 p.m. Then they had three more feeds during the evening up till about 11.30 p.m. When a youngster was presented with a fish it grabbed it and swallowed it hungrily. There was no need at all for force-feeding after the early stages when they had been so weak. Sometimes one or two of the youngsters would not eat at all, and we would put them apart till the others had finished. If the bird did not take the fish the next time it was offered we assumed that it was in the process of ejecting a pellet, and it seemed that they would never take fish till they had rid themselves of the remains of the previous meal. Next time the kingfishers who had refused the food took more than their fair share. Soon we found that the feeding times could be reduced to five times a day: 8 a.m., 12.30 p.m., 5.30 p.m., 8 p.m. and 10.30 p.m. Each bird ate its fill, a large bullhead or two small ones, or three or four sticklebacks. Sometimes minnows were available and the birds relished these.

We were now very busy catching food for this ever-hungry family. More than ever before kingfishers were reliant upon our ability to catch fish. We had to be up early every morning, and sunrise would find us wandering about the cressbeds in search of a new supply of fish, and at nightfall too we would wearily return with a bucket of swimming fish. The worst of our troubles was to find a way of keeping the bullheads alive in captivity. We often found that they had died during the night and were then too stiff, a bit 'off' to feed to the youngsters. Eventually we found that the colder the water the more likely they were to survive and so it was not long before the bottom tray of the refrigerator became a bullhead reserve. We did not, however, feed these cold fish to the kingfishers straight from the refrigerator, but let them thaw out for a while before feeding.

Day by day the youngsters grew. Firstly their eyes opened. Then their feathers broke through in quills, and almost immediately a few of the quill cases split and some of the feathers emerged. By twenty-one days they were fully feathered and spent much time flapping about. At twenty-four days they would no longer stay in their box home for they could now fly, so we had to give them the freedom of a small room which we used as our workshop. Feeding time was very different now. Each bird had to be found, caught, and fed, though they did not show any objection yet to being handled. The churring noise they used to make when they were hungry had ceased and instead they adopted a single chirp. This is the time when they would normally have left the shelter of their nest and sought their fortune in the big outside world, but we were reluctant to let them go until we were sure that they could look for and catch fish for themselves. We knew that the parents usually help them the first few days until they can get enough food themselves. This time there would be no parents to keep the birds from starvation point and we decided that before we let them go they must learn to fish. Also if they were to learn we would not have to feed them. So on their twenty-fifth day they were left all day to watch some fish swimming about in a shallow bowl. We counted the fish before we left them, and at lunchtime none had been taken. There was still the same number in the bowl in the evening and, thinking they were not yet developed enough to fend for themselves, we gave them a good feed. They seemed to have no idea that the fish were for them to catch and eat, for they sat looking at the ceiling in the most unkingfisherlike manner.

Slowly the birds caught on to the fishing technique and we would throw the fish down on the floor. Soon some of them learned to go and fetch them. The next step was to exchange the dead fish for live ones and immediately the birds ignored them, though to this day I cannot see why. By the twenty-seventh day they would sit over the bowl from time to time and watch the fish swimming about, making no effort to catch any of them.

We realised that we would have to be ruthless and not feed them regularly, so that they would have to fish when they became really hungry. But still they would not do so and we resorted once again to feeding them, since we did not want to see all our good work undone.

We thought they might be aroused by hearing their parents calling, so we played back our tape-recordings. As a last resort we sat them all along the shoe-box that had been their home and showed them film of their parents fishing. We played the calls as well. Although they watched the long shots with some interest (for these shots were in proportion to their own size) they lost interest when the screen was filled with what must have seemed to them monsters—their parents in close-ups.

No sooner had we run out of ideas than two of them

seemed to grasp the fishing technique. The great day came when one who had spent a long time watching the fish actually jumped in and made a catch. This seemed to stimulate one of the others, and soon two of them were able to fish. Then the inevitable happened. We had always been careful to close the door behind us, but the recent exciting events must have made us careless for we found on the next visit that one was missing. We searched the room high and low, but there was no sign of the missing bird. We were at a loss to know what to do next when someone came and told us that a kingfisher had been seen flying over the house within the past hour. It must have slipped out behind us before we had shut the door, and flown out of our bedroom window.

Next day we watched up and down the river for it, and not only did we see it but we also saw the cock bird feeding it, which must have been strange for him since his mate was then incubating another clutch of eggs.

With him looking after them they might stand a chance of surviving after all and the next day, a Sunday, we let the two that could fish go. It was a warm morning, and we released them in the garden, which is only seventy-five yards from the river, and saw them disappear towards the sidestream near the cressbeds. We were inclined to think that we ought to have released them all and so, hoping that the cock bird might find them to feed them all, we took the others across to the river and let them go too. It was only a short while after they had fluttered off we realised our mistake. They had no idea of fishing at all. They still sat looking up in the air instead of down at the water, and only ten minutes later one that had flown upstream got into trouble. The cock bird attacked it and it now came floating downstream flapping about in the water. Presumably the cock had tried to drown it and the strong current had carried it away. We rescued it and recaptured another which was sitting quietly in a bush opposite. We took them back home and built a pool in the greenhouse for them, which we stocked with fish. We were determined they should remain there till they could fish and become strong enough to fight.

By noon, after searching for the others, we found the first dead one. Whether it had died as a result of drowning through too frequent wetting whilst trying unsuccessfully to fish, or whether the cock had attacked it, we did not find out, but in front of us lay three and a half weeks of hard work and care by us, now but a sad handful of wet feathers in a pool of weeds.

There was still one to be recaught and this spent most of the day in the lower branches of a bush. It had caught nothing as far as we knew, and that night it roosted in the same place. Ron crept up to it and caught it, and it was soon enjoying a hearty meal. It settled down for the night in the greenhouse with the other two.

After a few days two of them seemed to get the idea of fishing, although the third one still had to be fed. When we fed them they had always come when we had called and taken the fish we offered, but once they had learnt to fish for themselves they grew aggressive when we appeared and often went into hostile stances. Often they would fight each other for the fish they had caught. The third one had some idea of catching fish for he would get down into the pool on the greenhouse floor and would catch the fish near the edge of the pool. He had no idea of keeping dry and would waddle about in the shallow water trying to catch the fish more in the manner of a heron. We dried his feathers at least three times a day with the hair-drier, but eventually he died, probably of pneumonia.

A fortnight later, when the birds were six weeks old, we let the two remaining youngsters go. They were strong enough then to fight their own battles, and they could fish excellently. Another fortnight passed during which we saw nothing of them; then one day, whilst talking to some of the cressbed workers, we learned that two young kingfishers had been found dead amongst the cress. These could have been two of the second brood, who would have been fledged by then, or they could have been two of ours. We never discovered which. If they were two of ours we had the satisfaction of knowing that at least two of our six had survived, and this at least wasn't too bad.

The kingfishers were never actually tame when we had been feeding them, although they had come when we called. Probably we could have tamed them more if we had tried, but this is the wrong attitude to take with birds that one eventually intends to release. We were sorry to be parted from them, and even sorrier to think that four of them might have perished, though the same fate happens to any brood of birds. It was good to think that at least we had sent two kingfishers out into the world who could safely look after themselves.

15

Final Touches

WHEN WE HAD finally released our hand-reared kingfishers we thought that our connection with the species
must be at an end. That year editing the film was
completed. In May the following year it was transmitted as a bird study on 'Look,' 3rd May, 1966, a
film with a 'family' story to entertain a general audience.
But this was still not the last of the kingfisher for us.
Many people now wanted to see the kingfishers and
some even wanted to photograph them. One enter-
prising gentleman wanted to try and take a stereo
(3D) picture. He tried several times at our stream but
failed to get a picture through technical hitches.
Eventually he took to pursuing the kingfishers of the
River Loddon where he made his own kingfisher 'set.'
If we were given enough time beforehand we were
able to bait one of the streams with our kingfisher bird-
table so that visitors could get a good view of the birds.
If this proved impossible many a long hour was spent
waiting in the precincts of the bottom of the cressbeds for the briefest glimpse of a kingfisher. On one
occasion after waiting over two hours near one of the
kingfishers' favourite perches, we were informed by

the waterkeeper that we could have seen the kingfisher if we had gone on to the top of the cressbeds, where he had been watching one fishing for some considerable time.

We had taken only a few still photographs of the kingfishers during the time we had been filming, and we took these for the record because we thought they would be unique. These showed the kingfishers being fed in the nest and the parents with fish in their beaks ready to feed. Soon after the film was transmitted we were asked for a set of kingfisher photographs, including one of the kingfishers catching fish underwater. We started to make some new sets to meet the demand. Since the pictures were wanted urgently we set the aquarium up in a stream in the cressbeds. The tank with the perspex front was placed in the stream with the front facing south, and we knew from the white-washed stinging nettles under the elder at the back of the tank that this was probably a favourite fishing and resting place of the kingfisher. The tank was arranged exactly as it had been for filming, with the fish lying at the bottom. For a day or two we kept the water-level down and were encouraged when the fish began to disappear. The camera we used, a 250 mm. lens on an Exacta Varex, was such that the hide would have actually to be in the water. So on the third day, with the tank filled to the brim and the water of the stream flowing between our feet, we settled in the hide in the hope of getting some pictures. We anticipated a long job for there was a lot of luck needed to get the bird both exactly in the right place in the frame and at the same time actually in the act of seizing its prey. With High Speed Ektachrome at 1/1000th of a second we hoped that we might stop the action. We discovered that the best way to take a picture was to line the camera up on a 6 in. × 8 in. area of the tank and watch out of the peephole of the hide, ready to press the cable release when the kingfisher hit the water.

We had not long to wait before the first kingfisher came upstream and landed opposite us. We could tell that it was a juvenile cock from his actions and his appearance, although he was already moulted. He seemed rather reluctant to dive into such deep water, although from his perch in the elders he could see several juicy bullheads. In fact the bird made several attempts at diving before he eventually gave up. The water was a lot deeper than he had been used to. Possibly he had learnt from early experience, similar to the one that some of the youngsters had had when attempting the mill pool.

After he had flown away 'empty-handed' we settled down to wait for another kingfisher to arrive or for the first one to return. It was not long before we heard a call and, peering out of the viewing holes in the hide, we saw a hen bird sitting on the elder branch. We were not sure at first if it was our own hen for we had not seen her in close-up for such a long time, but after we had scrutinised her turning around on the perch we began to recognise the old features—the more upright posture, the long, straight bill (the cock's had been very slightly hooked at the base), and the coloration of her under-mandible (which is not necessarily the same in all hen kingfishers; in fact some are almost totally lacking the red coloration). Even if we had not recognised her by these features we should have done so by her fishing. It must have been nearly two years since she had taken a meal from the aquarium, but from the way she tackled that amount of water it might only have been yesterday. Hardly giving herself time to aim she was down upon the first bullhead. We snapped her, and she returned to the perch to devour the fish.

After a few more shots we began to get our timing better and provided that she was diving into the area showing in the viewfinder we began to think that we might have taken at least one good picture. Then the sun went in and we could not get enough light at 1/1000th of a second. However we did not miss any fishing pictures for she had now stopped fishing and begun to preen. Very slowly we loosened the pan and tilt-head and moved the lens till it was directly trained on her. With a different aperture and shutter-speed we were able to take some good preening shots. Later, when she had emptied the tank, she disappeared and we had to restock.

Our next actor was the old cock bird, who was a little cautious of the tank but eventually caught several fish. The birds never came to fish together, but would call to each other in passing. After the first three rolls of film had been processed we found that the result of sixty frames was about four acceptable stills, but none contained one of the bird actually closing its beak upon the fish. Some only contained the bird's beak breaking the water, others revealed a streamlined, stretched blue form heading for the bottom of the tank, yet others showed the bird with its beak open and nearing the fish. There were some of the bird turning and one with the bird's wings open as it 'swam' back to the surface. The rest were masses of air bubbles and blurs. Unfortunately the air bubbles leaving the bird's feathers marred many of the pictures, for it was impossible to distinguish what the bird was doing.

Since some of them were probably blurred because we had used a shutter speed of 1/500th instead of 1/1000th we decided that a constant artificial light source upon the tank, in addition to sunlight, might improve conditions. So our next step was to borrow several hundred yards of heavy-duty electric cable from a friend, and to lay it from our house across the meadow and cressbeds to the elder tree above the tank. Unfortunately the results of a further two rolls of film were disappointing since the artificial light seemed to light up even more of the air bubbles and also gave the gravel in the tank a very yellow cast even though blue filters had been used on the lights. After this the artificial light idea was abandoned and we had to resort to photographing on fine days.

After two or three more rolls had been exposed we managed to get the picture we wanted, and a very interesting one it proved to be. The bird had just caught the fish, the picture was more or less free of air bubbles, but most noticeable of all was the fact that the eye of the kingfisher showing in the picture was closed. This meant that the bird must have closed its eyes as soon as it entered the water: an exciting discovery, for it showed that the kingfisher catches a fish that it cannot see, relying purely upon the accuracy of its aim as it leaves the perch. It would seem that a lot more high-speed cine-photography could profitably be done upon the kingfisher.

With the photography behind us there was only one other important job remaining: namely to see that the kingfishers' bank was ready for nesting in the spring.

We find that it usually needs building up at least every other year. It was most interesting to discover that the success of our kingfisher bank inspired other people who owned parts of the Test so that, to date, there are about half a dozen banks built specially for the Test kingfishers, and some of them are used regularly. To build a kingfisher bank, iron stakes about 5 feet high are driven in at intervals along the front of the prospective bank, and 4-inch deep sheep-wire mesh is fastened to them. The earth is then piled behind to a height of about 4 feet and a width of 3 to 4 feet; it does not fall through the wire to any great extent since the wire holds it back and incidentally also stops erosion of the bank by frost in the winter. Some kind of protection against small predators should be placed along the back of the bank, and we find that small mesh chicken-wire serves this purpose best. The 4-inch mesh along the front of the bank is about the right size for the kingfisher to get through and makes a convenient perch for them whilst they start their excavations. The main consideration in the choice of nesting place must of course be seclusion. Hence it is wiser to choose the bank of a side stream rather than that of a main river. Since the Test does not have many high banks on either the river or its streams much more of this type of work is called for, and the trout fisherman who encourages the building of banks and accepts the kingfisher is doing a very fine job in the preservation of our most attractive bird species.

We know now that the kingfisher is easy to find and among the easiest of birds to photograph, once the places they are likely to frequent have been discovered. I still remember how we used to search the riverside only a few years ago to try and find their nests, and how we would try to follow the kingfisher as it vanished rapidly along its flight path in the hope that he might reveal to us where he had hidden his family. The way in which we attracted them to our bird-table to fish and to the bank to nest, proved to be by far the easiest way of studying them. Some people might say that we did not get a true picture of their lives. I can only say that the kingfishers never saw us and so were never pressed into doing something unnatural.

The one real regret we have was that we were only able to spend evenings, week-ends, and selected holidays watching them, instead of whole days and weeks on end. Because of this it is likely that there is still more to be discovered about the bird, although we captured upon film the most intimate parts of its life. The aggressive sequence was the only inconclusive material we shot, and probably if time and money had allowed we could have filmed this elsewhere, perhaps on the Continent on the kingfisher's migratory routes, where fights often occur. The other regret was that the film was shot on 16 mm.; had we used 35 mm. the quality would have been better.

Until this year, 1968, we had never found where the kingfishers roost. We had always imagined that they went to roost in the ivy of a tall elm in the cressbeds. Early this spring the tree was brought down in a storm. One June evening at dusk, I was taking the dog for a walk through the cressbeds by the river. Once the openness of the cressbeds was behind us we rounded a part of the river which is lined with tall alders. Some of the smaller ones, as yet bushes, overhang the river. It was very quiet as all the song-birds had gone to roost, and it was only just light enough to see. I paused to watch some young coots in the rushes opposite; the dog made a snorting noise as it nosed the grass, a noise which must have disturbed the occupant of the alder bush near the coots, for as I looked up the small blue form of a kingfisher slipped out from amongst the leaves and silently and swiftly disappeared upstream and into the night.

We see very little of the kingfishers now though we are assured by an occasional whistle that they still live in this area. For as long as the waters of the Test remain pure there is reasonable hope for the bird's continued survival. On a depressing winter's day there is a certain enjoyment to be found by the streams of the Test, when the little blue halcyon bird can be seen flying fast downstream in search of a quick meal before the last light of the short day fades.

References

D. A. BANNERMAN: *The Birds of the British Isles.* 1953-63. Edinburgh: Oliver and Boyd

P. BARRUEL: *Oiseaux 21* (Speed of flight)

R. L. BROWN: *British Birds 27* (Breeding)

P. S. BURNS: *British Birds 27* (Display)

P. A. CLANCEY: *British Birds 28* (Egg-destroying habits. Unusual brood)

W. E. COLLINGE: *Ibis 1921* (Economic status)

Country Life 1908 (pp. 258-9): Persecution of kingfishers by hatchery keepers

P. F. GOODFELLOW and P. J. DARE: *British Birds 38* (Display)

W. GRIST: *British Birds 27* (Robbing dipper)

C. HARE: *Bird Lore,* 1952. London: Country Life

J. W. HILLS: *The River Keeper.* 1947. London: Bles

N. L. HODSON: *British Birds 54* (Taking insects)

HELEN M. RAIT KERR: *British Birds 12* (Display)

M. MURRAY MARSDEN: *British Birds 21* (Display)

D. MASSEY: *British Birds 25* (Kingfisher trapped by frost)

W. P. PYCRAFT: *Story of Bird Life.* 1900. London: Newnes

J. T. R. SHARROCK: *British Birds 55* (Taking insects)

A. SINGER: *Birds of the World.* 1961. London: Paul Hamlyn

J. ELLIOTT STEELE: *Zoologist, 12.* 1908. (Nesting)

J. STEFFEN: *Oiseaux 22* (Combat)

H. STEVENSON: *Birds of Norfolk.* 1866

P. O. SWANBERG: *Var Fagelv 11* (Breeding)

C. B. TICEHURST: *History of the Birds of Suffolk.* 1932. Gurney

E. C. L. TURNER: *Broadland Birds.* 1924. London: Country Life

Index

Numbers in bold denote main text references

Index